D1476716

CORNELIUS CARDEW

I PLAY FOR TODAY

Editors

Kate Macfarlane

Rob Stone

Grant Watson

THE DRAWING ROOM

M HKA

SHREWSBURY COLLEGE LIBRARY

Inv No. I-113483 Date 19-4-10

Ord No. 32870 Date 18-3-10

Class No. 780.92 MAC

Price £18.00   Checked   T

060598

Cornelius Cardew (1936–1981) was an experimental British composer whose interests and activities both reflected and contributed to the breaking down of barriers between different disciplines that took place during the 1960s. Cardew's approach to life was dynamic – he constantly questioned, doubted, reassessed, and changed tack. This character trait caused him to change the forms in which he realised ideas, from traditional musical notation, through to abstract shapes, diagrams, written instructions, personal journals and published writing, actions and song lyrics, and finally to militant action and political campaigning.

Cardew began his book *Stockhausen Serves Imperialism* (1974), in which he virulently attacks not only the music of John Cage and Karlheinz Stockhausen but his own, with the statement 'This book raises more questions than it answers.' The Cardew exhibition that Grant Watson curated with Adrian Rifkin at M HKA, in summer 2008, was staged in the manner of a question. The questions and contradictions inherent to Cardew's diverse practice have been pursued, in collaboration with Grant and Rob Stone, in *Play for Today: Cornelius Cardew*, this book and a symposium at the ICA, as well as though *Cornelius Cardew: Play for Today*, an exhibition at The Drawing Room.

The exhibition, *Cornelius Cardew: Play for Today* re-presents archival material, some of which is reproduced in this book. This is a selection of the various forms of graphic expression that were vital to the development of Cardew's ideas, from the pure graphic forms of *Treatise*, through to diagrams and visual instructions, letters and transcripts of discontent, song lyrics and finally to the more functional agitprop role of graphics as the conveyer of political message. In the last decade of his life, Cardew regarded his earlier projects as irrelevant to the cause of the 'class struggles surging around us in the imperialist heartlands of today'.[1] In 1976 he denounced *Treatise* as a 'disease of notation, namely the tendency for musical notation to become aesthetic objects in their own right.'[2] So can we justify presenting it as just that? *Treatise* could be seen as the gateway for Cardew's quest to invest avant-garde music-making with a political dimension. He began this project in 1963 in the belief that these visual forms were the answer to creating a score that would release the performer from the constraints imposed by traditional musical notation. The exhibitions and this book provide an opportunity for audiences to look again at this and other graphic scores. In the words of John Tilbury, *Schooltime Compositions* (1967) 'encapsulates Cardew's philosophy of musical education: the world as material for musical composition; and the moral dimension of music as an expression of human relations'.[3] The *Nature Study Notes* bring together the 'Improvisation Rites' composed collaboratively by Scratch Orchestra members: 'An improvisation rite is not a musical composition; it does not attempt to influence the music that will be played; at most it may establish a community of feeling, or a communal starting-point, through ritual.'[4] These Rites are referred to as 'Nature Study Notes' because the exercise book they were gathered in bore this title. The 'Scratch Books' kept by Scratch Orchestra members resemble the artist's sketch book, a place where new, unresolved and fleeting ideas are captured and stored for later use. The principles that informed these different graphic expressions never went away. They simply found different forms.

It has been a privilege to work with members of the Scratch Orchestra and Cardew's family – Stella, Horace and Walter Cardew – in the development of the project. John Tilbury, in particular, has contributed enormously, and the paper he delivered at The Drawing Room in July 2009 is included in this book. Also included is Michael Parsons's informative essay, 'The Scratch Orchestra and Visual Arts'. During 'From Scratch: A Forum', which took place at The Drawing Room on 2 July 2009, the 40th anniversary of the first Scratch Orchestra meeting, Cardew's sons Horace and Walter performed a new work inspired by Scratch music, Eddie Prévost talked about introducing Cardew to improvisation through the AMM group and Laurie Scott-Baker performed a work that included excerpts of the last public speech made by Cardew. Scratch Orchestra member Caroline Finer donned a special outfit and distributed party paraphernalia to recreate the spirit of a Scratch Orchestra happening. Attendees, of all generations, were predictably discomforted by this call for participatory action. This event constituted history colliding with the here and now, a suitable starting-point for the lively discussion that ensued, artfully steered by Andrea Phillips, whose incisive essay for this book similarly navigates an interesting course between Cardew's ideas and contemporary practice.

The book includes two contemporary projects. In *Communists Like Us (Towards Otolith II)*, Anjalika Sagar and Kodwo Eshun spin a rich historical web prompted by a voyage taken by Sagar's grandmother to Mao's China. The staging of this work included 'Paragraph 2' of *The Great Learning*. Cardew's utopian conception of this Paragraph, which required a large number of trained and untrained voices, instigated the formation of the Scratch Orchestra. The irony of this radically democratic collective enacting the ethos of Confucianism, which Cardew himself questioned very shortly afterwards, is highlighted through this work by the Otolith Group.

The Cardew Object is a project by the international collective Ultra-red in collaboration with *School of Echoes* (London). Cardew struggled to reconcile his considerable artistic talents with the rampant injustices of the world and his politically motivated activities were seen as a rejection rather than advancement of the aesthetic avant-garde. Ultra-red's activities encompass participation, subjectivity and the aesthetic object in a bid for emancipation at a more fundamental, structural level.

Play for Today: Cornelius Cardew, the book and symposium, have been generously funded by Middlesex University. The designer, Marit Münzberg, has worked tirelessly to produce

a concept that fits the complexities of this project. We would like to thank Dave Smith and John Tilbury, for co-ordinating the performance of *Autumn '60*, and 'Paragraphs' 3 and 6 of *The Great Learning* for the symposium. The Drawing Room 'From Scratch' series of events was conceived in collaboration with Claire Macdonald and Chris Ralls of the International Centre for Fine Art Research (ICFAR), University of the Arts, London. Paula Naughton, our Administrator, played a key role in the conception of the series; we would like to express our gratitude for this and for her considerable contribution to The Drawing Room.

M HKA and The Drawing Room would like to thank Horace Cardew, Brigid and Laurie Scott-Baker and Carole Finer for their generous loan of precious archival material. Adrian Rifkin's vision, and Celine Vandendriessche's hard work to realise the exhibition at M HKA, are gratefully acknowledged. We would also like to thank: the musicians who performed at M HKA, July 2008, including Champ d'Action (Stefan Prins, Ann Eysermans, Kris Delacourt, Maarten Buyl, Serge Verstockt, Thomas Olbrechts, Peter Verdonck, Matthias Koole) and Alvaro Guimaraes with the Novecanto Choir; those who performed *Treatise* at The Drawing Room, July 2009 (Angharad Davies, Rhodri Davies, John Lely, Tim Parkinson, Lee Patterson and James Saunders); Mark Sladen and Richard Birkett of the ICA and participants in the symposium – Lawrence Abu Hamdan, John Levack Drever, the Otolith Group (Kodwo Eshun and Anjalika Sagar), Dr Andrea Phillips, Adrian Rifkin, Dieter Roelstraete, Dave Smith, Rob Stone, Marcel Swiboda, John Tilbury, Ultra-red and Grant Watson.

1   Cornelius Cardew, 'Stockhausen Serves Imperialism', in Eddie Prévost (ed.), *Cornelius Cardew (1936–1981): A Reader* (Harlow, UK: Copula, 2008), p.151.

2   Cornelius Cardew, 'Wiggly Lines and Wobbly Music', *Studio International*, no.984, vol. 192, Nov/Dec 1976, anthologised in ibid., p.249.

3   John Tilbury, *Cornelius Cardew (1936–1981): A Life Unfinished* (Harlow, UK: Copula, 2008), p.372.

4   Cornelius Cardew, 'A Scratch Orchestra: Draft Constitution', 1969.

A large number of enthusiasts come together. They pool their resources and form a collective involved in the spontaneous enjoyment of music and, in the process, give rise to all sorts of experimental activities. They address the public directly through concerts in traditional music venues, but also community centres, village halls in Cornwall and Wales, as part of anti-nuclear demonstrations, in university auditoriums, at protests and in the forecourt of Euston Railway Station. They produce their own scores from the ephemera of daily life, using illustrations cut out of newspapers and magazines, advertisements, artwork by children, doodles, short and simple instructions, hand-drawn diagrams. They develop research projects and they invent their own private journeys. They are also active at macro- and micro-political levels participating in direct action but also using their music to work on group dynamics. Old footage of rehearsals from television programmes, produced by the Arts Council and the BBC, show the group doing this in a free-flowing and idiosyncratic manner that would not be tolerated today. Their scores are often works in themselves, for example, a page from Cornelius Cardew's *Nature Study Notes* is a collection of loose sheets, folded and stuck one on top of the other, each sheet an elegant haiku with the potential to activate music. They create a framework, written down as a Draft Constitution – a sort of meta-score that sets the rules but leaves a wide margin for interpretation.

Looking back at the Scratch Orchestra after 40 years, it seems hard to pick an argument with any of this, but like most quasi-utopian projects, it germinated its own contradictions. Unrest in the orchestra produced a document circulated under the title 'Discontent', which led to the organising of Discontent Meetings and the soul-searching and self-criticism that followed provide fascinating reading.[1] Taken from the minutes of meetings, public talks, Cardew's notes and his book *Stockhausen Serves Imperialism*, they raise questions about politics and culture, accessibility, audiences, responsibility and self-indulgence, criticality and transformation. The collective tone is a mixture of serious analysis, bitchy and humorous critique, humility, and text-book Marxism. A document called 'Art for Whom?' sums up the situation towards the end of the life of the orchestra.[2] That this title sounds like a current Arts Council report shows how these questions persist, while the language inside has a directness that transports us to a completely different era. It begins: 'We in the Scratch Orchestra want our art to serve the people. In trying to put this into practice, we've found that it is not as simple as it sounds.' It continues: 'The orchestra began as an experimental music group, its aim was to change the traditional forms of music so that anyone, whether musician, painter, bank clerk, teacher, student or labourer could participate. This was a reaction against the elitism existing in the classical and avant-garde music circles. We found, in practice that what we wanted to achieve did not happen. What actually happened was that only a handful of people wanted to hear us play, and most of those who did come left well before the end of the performance.'[3] Cardew's own words from this time run into a whole book on the subject of his past mistakes, which he traces back in part to his training with Karlheinz Stockhausen. The section on *The Great Learning* is interesting because it addresses, in detail, the ideological implications of what is perhaps his most famous score (the Scratch Orchestra was in part established in order to play *The Great Learning*). The libretto, a scripture by Confucius (translated by poet and fascist-sympathiser Ezra Pound) in a more ideological moment has become an embarrassment, a blend of mysticism and conformity and the choice of a 'politically backward composer wrapped up in the avant-garde'.[4] Unable to abandon *The Great Learning* completely even as he describes it as 'a piece of inflated rubbish'[5], Cardew first tries to reform the work then changes his mind, saying that 'a reformed Great Learning can never be more than an armour-plated butterfly'.[6]

The Scratch Orchestra's record is evaluated in Rod Eley's 'A History of the Scratch Orchestra 1969–72' which constitutes the first chapter of *Stockhausen Serves Imperialism*. In it, Eley describes the original character of the orchestra during its 'golden age' as being a 'social body', which in a 'blind way' knew that it had 'some functional role in present day social change', in part through the search for some method of 'organising people to a common task without infringing their individuality'.[7] He relates how sections of the orchestra began to question this approach in favour of a clear-cut political alignment and how the issue of audience came to the fore, in particular the orchestra's lack of proletarian support. Eley puts forward some successes such as the tour of village halls which took place during July and August of 1970, where the orchestra played to an audience of the 'rural proletariat'. Here 'the reception was friendly and good natured by people who had not heard of Cage or Stockhausen. People joined in and played with the Scratchers.'[8] But this is then negatively contrasted with what he describes as 'the fiasco' at the Metro Club, Notting Hill, on 12 June 1971, where 'we were faced with a club for young immigrants, oppressed by the bourgeois ruling class and therefore the natural enemy of capitalist society. There had been several arrests in a riot with the police at the club the previous week and there was a display board of telegrams and messages of support from the black liberation movements the world over. What did the Scratch Orchestra produce? *A Toy Symphony* – a typical Scratch

atavism, return to childhood. We experienced at last the true nature of our almost total incompetence.'[9]

Of course, the debates within the Scratch Orchestra did not occur in isolation but were part of broader changes taking place in society. Cultural life in London during this period is brilliantly satirised by Hanif Kureishi in his novel *The Buddha of Suburbia*, with the author lampooning attempts by middle-class cultural producers to give their works real-life efficacy. The story relates how Kamir Amir, a mixed-race teenager from the suburbs, born of two 'old histories' with an English mother and Indian father, makes his way 'in search of trouble' or indeed 'any kind of movement', from Beckenham in South London with its world of Asian corner shops, yoga classes, soft drugs, school bands, hippy die-hards and racist violence, to central London, where he gains success as a performer on the fringe.[10] Here he finds himself required to act out the issues of race and class that on a regular basis affect his relatives back in the suburbs. In the novel, the interplay between everyday experience and the artificial world of the stage produce a number of comic vignettes. During rehearsals, it turns out that the woman scrubbing the steps of a house near to the rehearsal room is the mother of fellow actress Tracy, and so the director invites her in during the lunch break to speak to the cast about her experiences as a cleaner. More seriously, on the night that Kamir is previewing a play in the West End and raising laughs with his impersonation of his friend Changez (who has recently arrived from Bombay to marry his cousin Jamila), he gets a call to say that his friend has been attacked under a railway bridge by a gang of thugs 'who jumped out on Changez and called him a Paki, not realising he was Indian. They planted their feet all over him and started to carve the initials of the National Front into his stomach with a razor blade.'[11] Disgusted, Kamir decides to join his cousin on a protest against a National Front rally outside the town hall the following Saturday. Musically the backdrop to *The Buddha of Suburbia* (and even more so the 1993 TV adaption of the novel) charts the shift from early 1970s rock – The Faces, Hendrix, Emerson Lake & Palmer through David Bowie (who is also from Beckenham) to the emergence of punk – providing a barometer of 1970s youth culture, and more generally the shift in social attitudes from freewheeling at the beginning of the decade to confrontational at its end. In his 1978 diatribe against the Queen's Silver Jubilee, which had taken place the previous year, Cardew refers to punk when he mistakenly clubs together *God Save the Queen* by the Sex Pistols (with its Union Jack poster) with the *Jubilee Hymn* by Malcolm Williamson and John Betjeman – as attempts to persuade the British public to support the monarchy.

Perhaps Cardew's mistake was understandable. In his portrait of the writer David Widgery, who was one of the founders of Rock Against Racism, David Renton describes how at this time the National Front was busily recruiting members and making headway at the ballot box in areas with large immigrant populations such as Hackney South and Bethnal Green, building a following amongst football supporters and the young unemployed, and how one of the battle-lines was music. Renton recalls: 'The National Front attempted to tap into this new punk style. They were helped by traces of ambiguity which punk displayed towards fascism. The style was anachronistic but politically vague and individualistic. The sound of punk, with its jagged three-chord repetitions, was the antithesis of 1970s reggae; in Jon Savage's phrase, 'The style had bled Rock dry of all black influences.' Members of the Sex Pistols wore swastikas, as if it could be a fashion statement, while one of their last singles pronounced that 'Belsen was a gas.'[12]

Renton describes how the campaign orchestrated by Rock Against Racism went on to be one of the rare success stories of the Left during that decade, in terms of the immediate effect it had on the National Front, which lost considerable support in the 1979 general election, as well its long-term impact on attitudes in British pop music and youth culture, where racism became, for the most part, unacceptable. Rock Against Racism was proactive and didn't 'simply adapt itself to the existing punk sound. Rather it sought to change and develop punk music. RAR brought together white punks and black reggae acts, Jimmy Pursey with rasta group Misty in Roots.'[13] Cardew's strange hybrid protest music from this time, with its rock opera overtones as well as his beautiful renditions of Irish rebel songs, are a world away from the punk concerts and carnivals organised by Rock Against Racism, and it doesn't make sense to compare them, but it is clear that as an effort linking politics and music they were making common cause.

The political climate of that period now feels like history, too far back to be remembered clearly. But I can recall what happened next, which was that the Left took a beating under Margaret Thatcher's Conservative Government. On CND marches in London or mass demonstrations at Aldermaston and Greenham Common, the mood reflected the generally polarised and antagonistic character of British politics, with anger personally directed at Mrs Thatcher and released in the repeated chants of 'Maggie Maggie Maggie Out Out Out.' These marches were tribal, with many disparate groups coming together to support the cause, including anarchists with black flags, hippy veterans of earlier campaigns, Quakers and other Christians, feminists and lesbians from the women's camp and members of the many Left factions of the kind to which Cardew belonged; often heavily proselytising their cause and handing out newspapers in the crowd. At the time, I found these newspapers alienating, with their tabloid-style rhetoric which seemed to me just like the right-wing red tops, only in reverse. Then recently I discovered some similar papers in a shop across the road from my flat on Wandsworth Road in South London called the John Buckle Bookshop. Run by members of the Revolutionary Communist Party of Great Britain (Marxist-Leninist) which in the past was affiliated to the Party of Labour of Albania, the shop was a time capsule, containing shelf-loads of the slim white volumes of Marx and Engels, which were in the past mass-produced in the Soviet Union and then distributed cheaply world-wide through a network of sympathetic agents. And here, amongst the leaflets denouncing American imperialism, illustrated pamphlets documenting infrastructural projects in North Korea and lots of books produced by the Communist Party of Canada (who were also somehow linked to the Albanians) on a half-empty revolving metal rack, I picked up a loose leaflet advertising a benefit concert by the composer Cornelius Cardew. This was in 2003, when I was just starting my research into Cardew and the Scratch Orchestra, so it felt like a happy accident. The character and location of the shop enhanced my interest by framing the composer within the once alienating, but now slightly exotic, context of unreconstructed Left politics from the late 1970s.

Perhaps because of his political affiliations, Cardew never went down as the celebrated figure in British cultural life that he might otherwise have done. An Arts Council documentary about Cardew made after his death, gives a chronological account of the composer's life, from his days at the conservatory in Cologne, to an anecdote by John Tilbury where he describes his last sighting of Cardew playing the piano in a community hall somewhere in Camden Town. It

reinforced the impression of a career separated in two, with the break marked by *Stockhausen Serves Imperialism*, which for some constituted the composer's fall from grace. Initially, because of this, I thought it would be good to focus on the second half of this equation in my research, until someone pointed out that what was more interesting than the pros and the cons of the early and late Cardew, were the questions being asked throughout – the way that the composer interrogated his practice, demanding that it have a meaningful place in the world – questions which for the Scratch Orchestra came to a head during the period of discontent. Subsequently, the various Cardew-related projects that I have worked on in collaboration with different partners, have tried to emphasise the continuity of this question, rather than the split between a before and an after.

So, in this spirit of enquiry, it is worth asking whom and what these Cardew projects are for? In terms of address, the audiences so far have been haphazard, dictated mainly by the various opportunities that have cropped up. In the process, Cardew's oeuvre has been presented in some unlikely settings, including an art fair and a museum in Belgium.[14] The first would have probably raised eyebrows amongst the original Scratchers (not to mention the later Marxists) who predictably denounced the commodification of culture and even treated public money coming from the Arts Council and the BBC with suspicion.[15] It could be argued that our radio programme about Cardew, that was broadcast from a community radio station located within the art fair, used its host like a Trojan Horse. As the conversation around the table picked up and we began to play snippets of music, the crush of people outside the booth (some looking in curiously, others rushing past) seemed to disappear, and we were speaking directly to an audience that was spread out across

London. The more political Scratchers might have seen this as just 'keeping the conversation going' and unfurled one of the banners (from the reformed version of *The Great Learning*) bearing the slogan – 'The revolution is not a dinner party.'[16] Presenting Cardew in a Belgian museum produced subtler forms of estrangement. Here, in several small rooms at the top of the building with windows overlooking a picturesque Flemish square, archival material, including musical scores, pamphlets, books, letters and political posters, were laid out in elegant old army vitrines, while speakers played a selection of Cardew compositions at low levels – simultaneously. The Scratch diagrams, instructions and graphic scores sat well enough, at home in the same building as the Fluxus antics of Ben Vautier and Robert Fillou, but the political posters, and issues of *Cogs+Wheels*, with their pragmatic and peculiarly British ugliness, seemed out of place. In particular, the anti-racist literature from the 1970s struck an odd note. Surely a more engaged project would have tried to activate this material in relation to the real and current fight against racism taking place outside in the city itself? One high point was the performance of 'Paragraph 1' by the Novecanto choir from Ghent, who chanted: 'The Great Learning takes root in clarifying the way wherein the intelligence increases through the process of looking straight into one's own heart'[17] – giving these lines a new character with their Flemish intonations. But the audience for this exhibition was scanty, the show went unnoticed in the press and at times it felt like this enterprise was simply the staging of my private foible. However, one visitor partly made up for this by coming almost every day. He required a personalised service, regularly calling me on the phone with questions, wanting to watch the film programme according to his schedule and requesting free CDs. Eventually he made his own programme, which was broadcast on Antwerp's independent station Radio Centraal. So after several incarnations, it feels good to present an exhibition in London's East End, with the involvement of ex-members of the Scratch Orchestra who figured in the debates outlined above, as well as, we hope, a new audience. When it comes to what these projects are for, there is no immediate answer. If Cardew demanded a clear-cut purpose from his practice and found it through an adherence to the Party, and Rock Against Racism – with its single aim and mass support managed to achieve its objectives – *Cornelius Cardew: Play for Today* constitutes a more modest proposition. If anything, reduced to its minimum, this could be described as a wish to present the material clearly, along with its inherent question content. A commission from the group Ultra-red demonstrates what can happen next. Namely, that people will apply what they see and hear to contemporary scenarios, taking principles borrowed from musical scores and methodologies gleaned from photocopied sheets and make them their own. And in the process rescue this from being an exercise in nostalgia.

1   Rod Eley, 'A History of the Scratch Orchestra 1969–72', Cornelius
     Cardew, *Stockhausen Serves Imperialism* (London: Latimer New
     Dimensions, 1974), p.22.

2   'Art for Whom?', text of talk originally entitled 'Art to Serve the People'
     written collectively by members of the Scratch Orchestra and given at
     the ICA on 25 January 1974.

3   Ibid., p.1.

4   Cornelius Cardew, *Stockhausen Serves Imperialism* (London: Latimer
     New Dimensions, 1974), p.97.

5   Ibid., p.101.

6   Rod Eley, 'A History of the Scratch Orchestra 1969–72', in ibid., p.19.

7   Ibid., p.19.

8   Ibid., p.21.

9   Ibid., p.22.

10 Hanif Kureishi, *The Buddha of Suburbia* (London: Faber and Faber,
     1990), p.3.

11 Ibid., p. 224.

12 David Renton, 'David Widgery: The Poetics of Propaganda', chapter 11
     of his *Dissident Marxism: Past Voices for Present Times* (London &
     New York: Zed Books, 2004), p.219.

13 Ibid., p.220.

14 The conversation on Cardew was part of *Enthusiasm*, produced by
     Project Art Centre, Frieze Projects and Resonance FM, 2006; the
     exhibition *Cornelius Cardew* took place at M HKA, Antwerp, Belgium,
     2008.

15 In his 'A History of the Scratch Orchestra 1969–72', Rod Eley dissects
     in detail the problems of accepting public funding.

16 Cornelius Cardew, *Stockhausen Serves Imperialism*, p.99.

17 Ibid, p.98.

A Scratch Orchestra: draft constitution

Cornelius Cardew

Definition: A Scratch Orchestra is a large number of enthusiasts pooling their resources (not primarily material resources) and assembling for action (music-making, performance, edification).

Note: The word music and its derivatives are here not understood to refer exclusively to sound and related phenomena (hearing, *etc*). What they do refer to is flexible and depends entirely on the members of the Scratch Orchestra.

The Scratch Orchestra intends to function in the public sphere, and this function will be expressed in the form of—for lack of a better word—concerts. In rotation (starting with the youngest) each member will have the option of designing a concert. If the option is taken up, all details of that concert are in the hands of that person or his delegates; if the option is waived the details of the concert will be determined by random methods, or by voting (a vote determines which of these two). The material of these concerts may be drawn, in part or wholly, from the basic repertory categories outlined below.

1 Scratch music

Each member of the orchestra provides himself with a notebook (or Scratchbook) in which he notates a number of accompaniments, performable continuously for indefinite periods. The number of accompaniments in each book should be equal to or greater than the current number of members of the orchestra. An accompaniment is defined as music that allows a solo (in the event of one occurring) to be appreciated as such. The notation may be accomplished using any means—verbal, graphic, musical, collage, *etc*—and should be regarded as a period of training: never notate more than one accompaniment in a day. If many ideas arise on one day they may all be incorporated in one accompaniment. The last accompaniment in the list has the status of a solo and if used should only be used as such. On the addition of further items, what was previously a solo is relegated to the status of an accompaniment, so that at any time each player has only one solo and that his most recent. The sole differentiation between a solo and an accompaniment is in the mode of playing.

The performance of this music can be entitled *Scratch Overture*, *Scratch Interlude* or *Scratch Finale* depending on its position in the concert.

2 Popular Classics

Only such works as are familiar to several members are eligible for this category. Particles of the selected works will be gathered in Appendix 1. A particle could be: a page of score, a page or more of the part for one instrument or voice, a page of an arrangement, a thematic analysis, a gramophone record, *etc*.

The technique of performance is as follows: a qualified member plays the given particle, while the remaining players join in as best they can, playing along, contributing whatever they can recall of the work in question, filling the gaps of memory with improvised variational material.

As is appropriate to the classics, avoid losing touch with the reading player (who may terminate the piece at his discretion), and strive to act concertedly rather than independently. These works should be programmed under their original titles.

3 Improvisation Rites

A selection of the rites in *Nature Study Notes* will be available in Appendix 2. Members should constantly bear in mind the possibility of contributing new rites. An improvisation rite is not a musical composition; it does not attempt to influence the music that will be played; at most it may establish a community of feeling, or a communal starting-point, through ritual. Any suggested rite will be given a trial run and thereafter left to look after itself. Successful rites may well take on aspects of folklore, acquire nicknames, *etc*.

Free improvisation may also be indulged in from time to time.

4 Compositions

Appendix 3 will contain a list of compositions performable by the orchestra. Any composition submitted by a member of the orchestra will be given a trial run in which all terms of the composition will be adhered to as closely as possible. Unless emphatically rejected, such compositions will probably remain as compositions in Appendix 3. If such a composition is repeatedly acclaimed it may qualify for inclusion in the Popular Classics, where it would be represented by a particle only, and adherence to the original terms of the composition would be waived.

5 Research Project

A fifth repertory category may be evolved through the Research Project, an activity obligatory for all members of the Scratch Orchestra, to ensure its cultural expansion.

The Research Project. The universe is regarded from the viewpoint of travel. This means that an infinite number of research vectors are regarded as hypothetically travellable. Travels may be undertaken in many dimensions, *eg* temporal, spatial, intellectual, spiritual, emotional. I imagine any vector will be found to impinge on all these dimensions at some point or other. For instance, if your research vector is the *Tiger*, you could be involved in time (since the tiger represents an evolving species), space (a trip to the zoo), intellect (the tiger's biology), spirit (the symbolic values acquired by the tiger) and emotion (your subjective relation to the animal).

The above is an intellectual structure, so for a start let's make the research vector a word or group of words rather than an object or an impression *etc*. A record of research is kept in the Scratchbook and this record may be made available to all.

From time to time a journey will be proposed (Journey to Mars, Journey to the Court of Wu Ti, Journey to the Unconscious, Journey to West Ham, *etc*). A discussion will suffice to provide a rough itinerary (*eg* embarkation at Cape Kennedy, type of vehicle to be used, number of hours in space, choice of a landing site, return to earth or not, *etc*).

Members whose vectors are relevant to this journey can pursue the relevance and consider the musical application of their research; members whose vectors are irrelevant (research on rocket fuels won't help with a journey to the Court of Wu Ti) can put themselves at the disposal of the others for the musical realization of their research.

A date can be fixed for the journey, which will take the form of a performance.

Conduct of research. Research should be through direct experience rather than academic; neglect no channels. The aim is: by direct contact, imagination, identification and study to get as close as possible to the object of your research. Avoid the mechanical accumulation of data; be constantly awake to the possibility of inventing new research techniques. The record in the Scratchbook should be a record of your activity rather than an accumulation of data. That means: the results of your research are in you, not in the book.

Reprinted from 'The Musical Times', June 1969

Example

Research vector	Research record
The Sun	29.vi. Looked up astronomical data in *EB* & made notes to the accpt of dustmotes (symbol of *EB*) and sunbeams
	1-28. viii. Holiday in the Bahamas to expose myself to the sun.
	29.vii. Saw 'the Sun' as a collection of 6 letters and wrote out the 720 combinations of them.
	1.viii. Got interested in Sun's m. or f. gender in different languages, and thence to historical personages regarded as the Sun (like Mao Tse-tung). Sought an astrological link between them.
Astrology	3.viii. Had my horoscope cast by Mme Jonesky of Gee's Court.
	etc

(note that several vectors can run together)
(the facing page should be left blank for notes on eventual musical realizations)

Spare time activity for orchestra members: each member should work on the construction of a unique mechanical, musical, electronic or other instrument.

APPENDICES

Appendix 1 *Popular Classics*
Particles from: Beethoven, *Pastoral Symphony*
Mozart, *Eine Kleine Nachtmusik*
Rachmaninov, *Second Piano Concerto*
J. S. Bach, *Sheep may safely graze*
Cage, *Piano Concert*
Brahms, *Requiem*
Schoenberg, *Pierrot Lunaire*
etc
(blank pages for additions)

Appendix 2 *Improvisation Rites from the book 'Nature Study Notes'* (two examples must suffice)
1 Initiation of the pulse
Continuation of the pulse
Deviation by means of accentuation, decoration, contradiction
HOWARD SKEMPTON

14 All seated loosely in a circle, each player shall write or draw on each of the ten fingernails of the player on his left.
No action or sound is to be made by a player after his fingernails have received this writing or drawing, other than music.
Closing rite: each player shall erase the marks from the fingernails of another player. Your participation in the music ceases when the marks have been erased from your fingernails.
(Groups of two or more late-comers may use the same rite to join in an improvisation that is already in progress.)
(blank pages for additions)
RICHARD REASON

Appendix 3 *List of compositions*
Lamonte Young, *Poem*
Von Biel, *World II*
Terry Riley, *in C*
Christopher Hobbs, *Voicepiece*
Stockhausen, *Aus den Sieben Tagen*
Wolff, *Play*
Cage, *Variations VI*
etc
(blank pages for additions)

Appendix 4 *Special Projects and supplementary material*
(blank pages)

At time of going to press, the orchestra has 60 members. More are welcome. A meeting to confirm draft constitution and initiate training should precede the summer recess. Projected inaugural concert: November 1969. Interested parties should write to Cornelius Cardew, 112 Elm Grove Road, London SW13.

Programme note

THE GREAT LEARNING

"Works of art that do not meet the demands of the struggle
of the broad masses can be transformed into works of art
that do". In the light of this statement by Mao Tsetung
we have embarked on the transformation of the Great Learning.
The aim is to present the work ~~as an example of~~ in process of
transformation rather than as a transformed object.
Confucius' text has been newly translated, the music of
paragraph 1 has been curtailed,ˣ slogans have been inserted
to link the work with the current situation; and a short
version of paragraph 2 included at the end.
Paragraph 1: The Great Learning means raising your level of
consciousness by getting right to the heart of a matter and
acting on your conclusions. The Great Learning is rooted
in love for the broad masses of the people. The target of
the Great Learning is justice and equality, the highest
good for all.
ˣ Slogans: Make the past serve the present. Revolution is
the Great Learning of the present. A revolution is not a
dinner party, it is an insurrection, an act of violence
by which one class overthrows another (Mao Tsetung).
Apply Marxism - Leninism - Mao Tsetung Thought in a living
way to the problems of the present.ˣ
Paragraph 2: We know our stand and so our aim is set.
Our aim being set we can appraise the situation.
We appraise the situation and so we are relaxed and ready.
We are relaxed and ready and so we can think ahead despite
all danger. Thinking ahead despite all danger we shall
accomplish our task.
    ˣ The 'stand' referred to in paragraph 2 is interpreted
as our class stand on the side of the working and oppressed
people. The 'aim' referred to is the overthrow of monopoly
capitalism and its replacement by socialism.ˣ

                    SCRATCH ORCHESTRA IDEOLOGICAL GROUP

Took this note to BBC. 8.8
Viewed RAH .9.8

Interview with Glock 15.8.
Version actually to be used after talking to Glock 15.8, excludes passages between xs
and includes a footnote: "This is an abbreviated version of a programme note
submitted by the Scratch 10 Group".

After leaving Glock I phoned back to ask that the following be added
"The BBC in accordance with its policy of not allowing the Proms to
be used as a political platform, has removed the political content
from the programme note & the performance".

Scratch Orchestra . 22.7.72.   Promenade Concert performance of The Great Learning #1

For this performance I have decided to curtail P1 to some extent, include a shorter, more disciplined version of P2, re-translate both texts & combine visually displayed slogans with the whistle solos. These changes represent an attempt to apply Mao Tsetung's remark in his Talks at the Yenan Forum on Literature & Art: "Works of art that do not meet the demands of the struggle of the broad masses can be transformed into works of art that do." The aim is to present the piece as an example of the process of transformation rather than as a transformed object.

New text for P1: THE GREAT LEARNING MEANS RAISING YOUR LEVEL OF CONSCIOUSNESS BY GETTING RIGHT TO THE HEART OF A MATTER AND ACTING ON YOUR CONCLUSIONS, ~~THIS ALSO PROVIDING AN EXAMPLE TO OTHERS~~.

THE GREAT LEARNING IS ROOTED IN LOVE FOR THE BROAD MASSES OF THE PEOPLE.

THE TARGET OF THE GREAT LEARNING IS JUSTICE AND EQUALITY, THE HIGHEST GOOD FOR ALL.

The slogans displayed with the whistle solos are:

1) MAKE THE PAST SERVE THE PRESENT
2) REVOLUTION IS THE GREAT LEARNING OF THE PRESENT
3) WORKS OF ART THAT DO NOT (etc as Mao Tsetung, above)
4) undecided, possibly 2 slogans, one addressing artists & the other addressing intellectuals (or educated people).

New text for P2 is on accompanying sheet. Please bring both sheets to rehearsals.

Procedure: P1 begins with stones & organ solo as usual. Then the approx equal groups of speakers & whistlers enter. The first slogan is displayed with the first whistle solo, etc, until the 4th whistle solo which may be a duet to match the fact that 2 slogans are displayed at that point. After this solo (duet) P2 begins, without any break. The new version of P2 is performed by 4 groups. Each group has a drummer & an instrumentalist, who takes over the role previously played by the lead singer. All the singers in a group sing the words in the same rhythm (agreed amongst themselves), & each note is long but not too long (say 8-12 secs).

Finance. Since others besides Scratch people will be taking part it seems best to divide the fee (? £300) equally amongst those taking part. I suggest we do this in cash out of Scratch Orchestra funds at the end of the morning rehearsal on the day of the concert. The organist gets a special fee from the BBC & so does the Musical Director (me).

Rehearsals: Sunday 6th August 6-8 pm ICA Gallery 3. This is for all mass effects: stones, speaking & whistling, singing in P2 (with instruments if available). At this rehearsal we shd decide whatever is still undecided about the performance, eg content of last 2 slogans, & the practical problems of presenting them visually on a large scale. We also need volunteers for some specialised parts that have not yet been filled.

Saturday 19th August 10-1. Albert Hall. 10 am drums & instruments only, P2.
  11 am. P2 Everyone
  12   P1. Stones, speaking, whistling.

Thursday 24th August 10-1 Albert Hall. 10 am Organ & visual slogans only
  11 am Everyone.

Performance: Thursday 24th August 9.45 pm Albert Hall. Programme also includes Stravinsky, Birtwistle, Bartok

| Organ: Michael Chant or John Tilbury | Whistlers: Greg Bright Alec Hill ? ? ? | Drummers: Gavin Bryars Penny Jordan Chris Hobbs Arthur Soothill | Instrumentalists: Alec Hill John White ? ? |

(not drums)

(also a few just to hold notes)   Suggestions or queries to C. Cardew, 112 Elm Grove Rd, SW13

17

Rod & Joy.
Kevin
Hugh
Adrian & Frances.
(Tim & Barbara)

CRITICISM OF MORLEY COLLEGE SCRATCH.

1 The Present organisation and methods of work at Morley College promote
the separation of theory and practice. *We don't know why we're doing these songs.*

2 Fundamentally it is based on a wrong analysis of the relationship of
revolutionary art to the revolutionary movement. *Investigated in vain rejected.*

3 The principal manifestation of this hiatus between theory and practice
is the liberal athmosphere prevailing at the Morley sessions.

In theory we uphold Marxism-Leninism, but we do not put the
Proletarian political line into practice.

We allow ourselves to be tutored by bourgeois experts; we have
nothing positive to learn from such experts. For example in theory
our principal task is to sing songs, but in practice the singing excercises
do not arise out of the problems encountered in the songs. The time
spent on excercises is out of proportion to the time spent on the songs.

The effect of this bourgeois line is to stop our progress on the
songs and promote reliance on experts and not proletarian self-reliance.
The bourgeois experts and the liberal athmosphere encourage us to do
both the singing and the physical excercises in a mechanical and unthinking
way.

The criticism of the political content of the songs is inevitably
reduced to academic and linguistic wrangles because it divorces the political
content from the music. *quibbles.*

We do not struggle in a proletarian politically conscious way to
establish the correct relationship between our artistic organisation and
the Party. Our reasons for wanting to play to the party are based on the
employee mentality.

This line has the effect of liquidating the role of revolutionary
art as a contributory factor to the growth of the mass movement.

We wish to start right now to put theory into practice with a
programme:

1. To analyse and repudiate bourgeois culture with a view to
developing English Proletarian Revolutionary Culture.
to destroy the old in order to bring forth the new.

2. What is the concrete manifestation of bourgeois culture
which oppresses us, which we must first overthrow before
we go forward? It is the line that we should wait for
an audience of 50,000 before we can begin to create art;
the line of self-cultivation, divorcing revolutionary art
from its dialectical relationship to the revolutionary
movement. *3. Raise level of political awareness.*

"Revolutionary literature and art are the product of the reflection of the
life of the people in the brains of revolutionary writers and artists."
(Mao Tsetung-Talks at the Yenan Forum part 2)

??

Art is not politics. The Party will not organise executive work. Ever.

ART FOR WHOM?

We want to discuss this because we in the Scratch Orchestra want our art to serve the people. In trying to put this into practice, we've found that it is not as simple as it sounds. Our lives, our art and the society we live in are all inter-related, we realised that we needed to examine all these three things very thoroughly. And in doing this we have learnt a great deal. We are very pleased to be giving this talk tonight because in writing it we have had to clarify our ideas and sum up what we have learnt so far, and in the discussion following, with your participation, suggestions and criticisms we hopeto learn a great deal more, and correct any wrong ideas we may have.

THE ORIGINS OF THE SCRATCH ORCHESTRA

In case some of you do not know what the orchestra is, or has been in the past, we would like to give a short outline of the Scratch Orchestra's development.

The Orchestra began as an experimental music group, its aim was to change the traditional forms of music so that anyone, whether musician, painter, bank clerk, teacher, student or labourer could participate. This was a reaction against the elitism existing in the classical and avant garde music circles. We found, in practice that what we wanted to achieve did not happen. What actually happened was that only a handful of people wanted to hear us play, and most of those who did come left well before the end of the performance; people were reluctant to participate, and when we did persuade them to, they would take over completely and everything got out of hand; new members would come along to meetings for a few weeks and then drift away; in casting off the traditional forms of music, we completely lost sight of what music is - to such an extent that anything could be called music, total silence, scraping chairs along the floor, banging stones together. To know how to play an instrument properly was considered a disadvantage; though we were a group, supposedly working together, members of the group performed as individuals, doing their own thing regardless of the group as a whole; ordinary people thought our music was meaningless, the only section of the public to take us seriously were the very elite we were rebelling against, that is to say, the Arts Council, the ICA, the music historians and the music critics. We found that we ourselves had forgotten the reasons for playing, our music became as meaningless for us as it was for most other people.

So by the middle of 1971, after two years of working together, these contradictions both within the orchestra and between the orchestra and the public had developed to such an extent that they could be ignored no longer. In a series of meetings and discussions, and with a great deal of struggle we started to thrash things out. The group divided, those who wanted to continue in the old way tried to stop the orchestra from ch nging its outlook, they failed and each went his own seperate way. Those who stayed together, guided by Marxism-Leninism-Mao Tse Tung thought, came to understand that our problems were not peculiar to us alone, but were shared in common by everyone in our society. The work which particularly helped us was Mao Tse Tung's "Talks at the Yenan Forum on Literature and Art". This society encourages us to put ourselves first, we have to promote ourselves, and secure good careers in order to attain a decent standard of living and to gain some security for the future. Lenin describes this life under capitalism very clearly, it is based, he writes, on the principal of "rob or be robbed: work for others or make others work for you: be a slave-owner or a slave. Naturally, people brought up in such a society assimilate with their mother's milk, one might say, the psychology, the habit, the concept which says; you are either a slave-owner or a slave, or else, a small owner, a petty employee, a petty official, or an intellectual - in short, a man who is concerned only with himself, and does not care a rap for anybody else.

If I work this plot of land, I do not care a rap for anybody else; if others starve, all the better, I shall get the more for my grain. If I have a job as a doctor, engineer, teacher, or clerk, I do not care a rap for anybody else. If I toady to and please the powers that be, I may be able to keep my job, and even get on in life and become a bourgeois."

Waltzing with Necessity

Adrian Rifkin

For an artist, it is not one's conscience, but one's talent, making cowards of us all. Cardew's courage to dismiss an earlier abstract artistry of his own is indeed heroic. His career bears a comparison to D. H. Lawrence. Both set aside an evocative use of the language of their medium for a kind of 'message' of sorts. John Cage in his own way did likewise. In this regard, Cornelius Cardew is not in bad company. However, it is in a work such as *The Great Learning* which I feel Cardew found a unique equanimity of means between a musical poetry and his political beliefs – something akin to what Christian Wolff is doing with similar concerns. As perhaps the last indigenous esoteric composer surviving on this planet, I deeply mourn Cardew's death. He wrote beautifully about my own music and played it exquisitely. Perhaps we are not that far apart than one might think. There will always be … Cornelius Cardew.

Morton Feldman, March 1982

As Feldman remarks, Cardew was an artist. There are, as yet, no other words for the phenomenon. Cardew knew this, what an artist is or should be was a vexed and troubling question of his moment – as it still is, but differently. Then, perhaps, the simple and stark division between the avant-garde and the revolutionary artist seemed like a habitable space, one well-furnished with historical disappointments and unfinished conflict. Restlessly, Cardew displaced here and there the problem of how else what he was, what he was fated to be, could be named or thought. He set it beside himself, as if beyond his control. In the graphic score, the instruction or the free association of the collective that he would motivate but not direct – the Scratch Orchestra, or a performance of *Schooltime Compositions*. He understood that it would be strange indeed if two performances from *Treatise* were to resemble one another. But if this were one

model for freeing the performer from the tyranny of the artist and the listener from the tyranny of performance, and both from the tyranny of comparison and expertise, then the democratic centralism of the Communist Party, to which he came to subscribe, was another model of an incommensurable freedom. Radically separate from the others it was a fully voluntary decision of servitude or sacrifice, of deliverance from the fear of the delusion of freedom through acceding to the necessity of class struggle and its 'inevitable' outcome in a dictatorship of the proletariat. 'Freedom is the recognition of necessity' … as Engels put it in his *Anti-Dühring*.[1]

In all of this, Cardew belonged to his time, to the protracted moment of transition to what came to be called postmodern culture, the instatement of the aporetic as a norm rather than the struggle for a definitive outcome or a specific truth. And while he decided to do battle for an outcome – a revolution – there can be little doubt that the cumulative influence of his work was, like that of other great modernists – John Cage, Nam June Paik, George Brecht – a profound inspiration for something other and contrary to that desire. And at the same time that his, and their, aleatoric and collective work so perfectly opened a perspective between some of the increasingly plural singularities of the time, together they had little meaning for the exponential flourishing of identities of otherness that was just to come – which, precisely, needed newly purposive aesthetics, just as they were to have little use for the priority of class struggle as the main aim (in the world today).

If, in this way, Cardew negated the negation, and then again, he disclosed not so much the possibility of transcending the musical avant-garde to which he belonged, but its immanence in each and every such gesture that he came to make; and he found, even if he did not recognise, that the activism of the one resembled the activism of the other, but only in contingency at the moment of performance. *Carpe diem*: on one day art and politics might look alike, but if the outcome could be predicted it could never be more than a tautology – something Zhdanov had hoped for in the closing years of Stalin's regime. So the day had to be daily seized if we were to blind ourselves to this, and making art in this way became too pragmatic. Look at the photographs of the comrades on their lorry, singing in the demonstrations; they look corralled, not free, artists under siege, a siege of their own invention. Necessity has got out of hand.

This relation of art and politics is, then, as much a matter of chance as the throwing of stalks to get a hexagram for the I Ching; the very notion is no more than a guide to contingency. So if Cardew turned his back on an acknowledged principle of chance in both composition and performance, the new chance, the chance taken by the political militant, was understood only as a matter of necessity. With each negation he negated, Cardew discovered how much we are enchained by the necessity of the chance in which we live. Cardew waltzed with negation, swift-footed and certain, and that's one reason he could be a kind of leader of the round. There could be no higher virtue than to denounce oneself, no skill more virtuously ratified, and if the true victim of his critique of Stockhausen was his self, a former self, then what he denounced triumphed again in the very virtuosity of his reflexive gesture. Psychoanalytically, this is the nervous gesture of an ill-founded and uncertain narcissism.

And it's true that, for a good Marxist-Leninist, sacrifice was at once the face of pure and disinterested love and the mask of an absolute and manipulative interest. The coincidence between a law of history and the interest of the exploited class meant this – that one was purely the instrument of this law and impurely for this class. And in straddling the narrow gap between a social agreement and a moral law (a gap so narrow that, in our time, art and politics can never pass through it hand in hand) perhaps – probably – we neglected the very material conditions that we sought to change, and which determine over and over the Janus figure of art and politics; of the freedom and servitude they owe to one another in order for the world so to be figured that we can begin to see where we are, and what we are.

That's why, I guess, that if Cardew was a great artist, he was a melancholy one, and the thread that binds him to Eisler in exile, the enraged defeated Schubert of 'Das Wirtshaus', and that turns in his hands into the perversely classical and astonishingly haunting beauty of his rewriting of Irish rebel songs, is the broken thread of defeat's unending. Or, this broken thread is the tradition of the avant-garde, its perfectly triumphant figure, and if – in Marx and Engels's phrase 'No country that enslaves another can itself be free' meant that the English revolutionary must first free Ireland, then Cardew's very aesthetic was bound by this thread to its own effacement, to becoming soundless, unvoiced – unless, that is, Ireland itself remain enslaved.

The more Cardew's later work pushes out into the figuring of the principles of revolutionary politics, the odder it becomes and the stranger its beauty. The closer he pushes it to a political objective, the more it seems to splinter into the oddity of a setting, the setting of an avant-garde modernism, to a political intrigue for which it was never destined to be more than a metaphor. And in this constricted space of misrecognition, there arises a new beauty (*Four Principles on Ireland*, for example) sometimes a banal clumsiness (*Smash the Social Contract*); and between them, they enable us to hear a warning and a lure, singing of the injustices in which we live today.

---

1   First published in Frederick Engels, *Anti-Dühring*; cited in Thomas A. Jackson, *Dialectics: The Logic of Marxism, and Its Critics – An Essay in Exploration* (New York: Lennox Hill, 1971 reprint of 1936 edition), p.593.

WHERE THERE IS OPPRESSION THERE IS

RESISTANCE

A Booklet of Anti-fascist Songs Old & New.

CONTENTS

Peoples' Liberation Music

REVOLUTION IS THE MAIN TREND

Revolution is the main trend in the world today (x2) The

danger of a new World War still exists & the people of all countries must get prepared, but

Revolution is the main trend in the world today

Ever since World War II, ever since World War II, U.S. imperialism and its followers have been con-

tinually launching wars of aggression & the people of various countries have been continually waging

revolutionary wars to defeat the aggressor. The danger of a new World War still exists & the

people of all countries must get prepared, but Revolution is the main trend in the world today

A new upsurge in the struggle against U.S. imperialism is now emerging throughout the

world. world. Revolution is the main trend in the world today.

CORNELIUS CARDEW

Four Principles on Ireland and other pieces (1974)

YOU ARE NOW ENTERING FREE DERRY

THE CROPPY BOY (2'47") / FATHER MURPHY (2'59") / FOUR PRINCIPLES ON IRELAND (3'52") / CHARGE (3'19") / SONG AND DANCE (2'16") / SAILING THE SEAS DEPENDS ON THE HELMSMAN (1'33") / BETHANIEN (4'02") / BRING THE LAND A NEW LIFE (4'12") / THE EAST IS RED (1'33") / RED FLAG PRELUDE (3'07") / SOON (there will be a high tide of revolution in our country) (2'07") / LONG LIVE CHAIRMAN MAO (1'58") / REVOLUTION IS THE MAIN TREND IN THE WORLD TODAY (3'18")

CRAMPS RECORDS/Milano

24

PUNK ROCK IS FASCIST!

During the past year the trend of 'Punk Rock' has been carefully nurtured and promoted to the youth, propagandising the ideology of pessimism, mindless aggression and violence, degeneracy and decay, racism, sexism, nihilism, blind rebellion and glorying in the symbolism and promotion of the Nazi movement. This is part of the entire process that has developed over the last two decades, when pop music has been used as part of an attempt to pacify and disarm the revolutionary sentiment of the youth. In the '60's there was a growing worldwide anti-imperialist sentiment reflected for example in the massive demonstrations in the West against the U.S. involvement in Vietnam and Cambodia, and most importantly in the Great Proletarian Cultural Revolution in China. It was no accident that the bourgeoisie at this time, promoted rock music and through it such trends as "Flower Power" and the "Hippy" movement with their cult of 'peace and love'. Nor is it suprising that such ideas as promoted on the Beatles song, "Revolution", released in 1969, were promoted;

"But if you go carrying pictures of Chairman Mao,
  You ain't going to make it with anyone anyhow".
Or these lines from "Street Fighting Man" by the Rolling Stones in 1968;
"What can a poor boy do 'cept that same old rock
                                and roll thing,
For sleepy London town is just no place for a
                          street fighting man."

4

Cogs + Wheels

"Proletarian literature and art are part of the whole proletarian revolutionary cause; they are, as Lenin said, cogs and wheels in the whole revolutionary machine."

Mao Tsetung: Talks at the Yenan Forum.

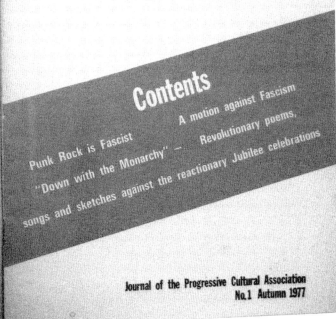

Contents

A motion against Fascism

Punk Rock is Fascist

"Down with the Monarchy" — Revolutionary poems, songs and sketches against the reactionary Jubilee celebrations

Journal of the Progressive Cultural Association
No. 1 Autumn 1977

INTERNATIONAL

WE SING f

Revolutionary songs, music and poems performed by
Committee and Performers from the West Indian Com

LONDON
SATURDAY, AUGUST 9

**Details to be
Announced**

BI
**7pm
RED LI
(opp
HA**

For further details write to: P

Organised by: PROGRESSIVE CULTU

CULTURE IN THE SERVICE OF

YOUTH CONCERT

FUTURE!

...*ltural Association, Canadian Cultural Workers'* ...*tain and Canada and the Indian community in Britain*

M ...ST 8 ...ROAD, ...d), ...1	**MANCHESTER** **6pm THURSDAY, AUGUST 7** **MEETING ROOM 1,** **MANCHESTER STUDENTS' UNION,** **OXFORD ROAD, MANCHESTER**

...Wandsworth Rd., London SW8.

...TION AND STALIN YOUTH BRIGADE

...PLE!   EVERYBODY WELCOME!

… it is impossible to record with any fidelity a kind of music that is actually derived in some sense from the room in which it is taking place – its shape, acoustical properties, even the view from the windows.

Cornelius Cardew, 'Towards an Ethic of Improvisation'

This swaying, this swing in which confused material goes about taking shape, is for me the only certainty of its necessity, because no sooner does it stop than I understand that I no longer have anything to say.

Julio Cortázar, *Hopscotch*

Old Habits, Old Customs (An Image of the People)

I recall seeing photographs of Cornelius Cardew in a duffel coat. It has a curious appeal, that innocuous, dislimning garment. There was a discrete moment in the British cultural landscape when it spelt out a threatening portent – one more considerable than that posed later by the donkey jacket, for instance, during the miner's strike, or those political excitements that were figured for other, earlier cadres by the M-65 field jacket, or even the Mao jacket. There was a time in the 1970s when the almost formless, untinted outlines of men and women made burly by duffels, huddled around braziers at factory gates, in interview, or marching and singing at rallies, really did look as if dramatic future changes in British society belonged to them.

The amorphising, collectivising effect of the duffel frightened some; and whilst news images seemed to conspire in this, the fear itself appeared for good and effective poetic reasons. Proof against neither wind, nor cold or rain, the duffel's texture, its prickling, heavy woollen cloth, seemed to speak itself about a kind of irresistible personal fortitude. There are qualities of miserable,

patriotic resilience in the duffel, too – the kind that Nicholas Monsarrat found for it with his naval tales. Especially where parlayed by cinema, these remained eloquent to a post-war audience. Stoical, grim persistence was then the essential British virtue, the still-vital stiffener of a simple capacity to endure that had helped achieve a European military victory. There was something about binoculars and command in there, cocoa and a desire to obscure oneself in rain and alcohol – perverse, but recognisable comforts. The rewards of that costly military victory, as it turned out, included national industries and a welfare state, not a resurgence of Empire. It isn't surprising then that the British middle classes of the 1970s – whose conception and experience of socialism and conservatism were cut in ways very different from today's – had trouble identifying what kinds of new social and aesthetic relationships, even class betrayals, their much-loved old coat now gestured towards. A cultural revolution, as well as political one, had appeared in the wind. In the 1970s, inasmuch as it had come to portray the sociable repose of labour in political combat (more than a simple index of labour itself), the duffel's shapeless form was a source of class anguish. This was for what it readily encoded, certainly, but also for its new receptiveness to further encryption and for the challenge to prevailing national fidelities that it vested. In the end, of course, the duffel didn't herald the change in political power it seemed to figure, and has since languished in its familiar morose habit – deject, occasionally prodded by fashion.

In that period of the 1970s, I didn't wear a duffel. I had an equally shapeless German army parka over the uniform of my Rhondda comprehensive school. Looking back, it doesn't feel as if I was working towards a rapprochement with Cardew then – though such a relationship was eventually, temporarily made; done, undone, redone. We couldn't have been more ignorant of, nor more dissimilar to each other. I knew his influence at a remove only. Or rather, put it like this, when BBC West broadcast footage of performances by the Portsmouth Sinfonia during the early 1970s (we received it via Rediffusion in South Wales), I knew enough to laugh with, rather than at, its social-aesthetic enterprise. Rather, my trajectory was in a coming to a love of The Fall, and an obtuse, naturally diffident politics; one very different to the too easily legible one by which I felt socially immersed. There was a want, widespread, to be less easily decidable.

So, I do my remembering of Cardew's coat with the kind of tinnient vividity (I love that sound) that makes me wonder if, in fact, the whole thing is just some necessary improvisation – an image that is plausible to me for what it is capable of metaphorising, constellating. That kind of unchecked memoir is more, well, libidinised, I suppose, more cathected, various, and more appreciable for that. There are pictures of Cardew, slim and purposeful in black shirt and blue jeans, I know. There are pictures of him speaking, lecturing, hectoring, in tweed, tank top and tie. Sometimes, there is a jacket, more like a blazer, and even a college scarf. There are lapel badges. I can't do anything about those. Recorded archival facts, they stand there, nearly malicious in their certainty. But, of all, certainty is the oddest sensibility to exercise around Cardew. Oughts or generalisations are equally so. Although Cardew may have had any number of relationships with what he understood to be the working class, it is important that he couldn't write a *Peter Grimes*. The oracular character of Grimes may indeed parallel the complicated proletariat that Cardew sought to realise. Yet, there is no programme music in his work, no fixed portrait – not even, and perhaps especially, in his later songs, where such a depiction seems impossible to deny. The ambiguities that are there are not like Britten's. They are not Shostakovian. They may not even be, strictly speaking, musical.

The approximate silhouette of Cardew's clothes, his habit, has a bearing on the music and all else that arose from the formal outline of his scores. Certainly there is a sense that these graphic remarks that are the subject of this exhibition, those on paper, as well as those made in politics and performance, don't actually care. They are not slovenly, far

from it. Neither are they uninterested or compromised. But, they represent no form of curatorial activity – at least, no conventional form. There might be some sense of hosting, but not quite hospitality. They do not appear to bend themselves towards a catered welcome. The marks that make up *Treatise, The Great Learning*, the Scratch pieces and so forth, may be read to find a distinction between the idea of improvisation (which foregrounds the performer) and interpretation which prioritises some composerly intention. At the same time, they might be read for signs of the way 'people', in Cardew's thought, started to separate out into the bourgeois and the proletarian. There is no invitation to this, though, no support.

This lack of care, or at least the pretence at it, is an affect that appears as an ungiving emotional hardness. It might be part of the ease, even eagerness, with which the concept of self-criticism appeared in Cardew's work around the early 1970s. To peer into a looking glass, prompted by the Mao of 30 years earlier, to see there only hideously contoured monsters seemed to be an almost delicious prospect. So, when it comes to looking at the forms of Cardew's scores, and the forms of self-recognition, the forms of social and aesthetic interaction that he and others may have had in mind for them, when it comes to thinking about class, autobiography and performed reflections upon these things, it is difficult to avoid a term like reification. For all the past bluster about instrumented social change, what now appears of renewed use is that Cardew gave both form, and the question of form, to a project of thinking through the necessary, preliminary experiments in perception, affect and sensibility that might lead to the production of uncommodifiable socio-aesthetic surpluses. This intellectual and emotional reconnaissance is what seems to matter. Charming things these surplusses, inhabitable, yet made at the liminal confluence of people's hopes, the traces of possible, uncharacterisable, unexploitable times of communication. They are sometimes indigestible and upsetting, and are things which, whilst they must themselves compel, possess no more than outline. Ghosts.

Old Ideas, Old Culture (In Dreams Begin Responsibilities)

It is genuinely amusing that investment bankers are able to promote the idea that they have some sense of social responsibility. Mainly, this is because it is probably true; more true there than in any elected civic forms. The profitable management of the interface between capital and industry brings with it a responsibility – admittedly not one frequently exercised – to tend: to optimise and lend communicable form to the surpluses, especially the relative surpluses that are produced by labour. Investment banking is, as Marx explained patiently, about the cultivation of the most useful forms of differentiation and micromanagement of time. The act of discriminating and fractioning different strands of time in labour is wherein lies profit. Through that procedure, as Marx put it, a kind of time which is various, flowing and approximate, human, becomes ossified, limited into a continuum filled with things – the formalised, objectivised, evaluable and negotiable products of both performed labour and of the labourer cut off from any sense of a broad, complex, contradictory and fulfilling existence. Time is turned into space in this way, a particular kind of recognisable, metrically dependable, bloodless space where the conceits, vanities and heroisms of lives are rendered secondary at best.

In 1972, Cardew went on national radio to accuse Beethoven of participating in this process. There is a rest – a fermata – in the score of Beethoven's Fifth Symphony. It comes immediately after the famous, four-note introduction. The fermata, insignificant enough as a mark, has a particular status. It is conventionally used in the concerto form to indicate an indefinable pause before the soloist's cadenza takes flight, if it is going to. In the Fifth, it is the instant of license given to the conductor, and only the conductor, to structure the character of the symphony's opening remarks in whichever way the conductor chooses, by deploying a silence. This is within the constraints of the received probitics of Beethoven performance practice. This is a moment of the articulation of the most profound gravity,

mood and grave human grandeur, when Saturn turns and lowers. In that moment, the performing musicians as people, with all their private, individual personal complications are effaced, reduced to their instruments, and more, the very acuteness of their command of their instruments is made to mock the musicians' condition of professional biddability, their utter lack of agency.

In his practice more generally, and in what else he was to say at this point, it seemed that Cardew would have liked to join Beethoven at this managerial interface between audience and performers, where profit is measured in staged emotional intensities and a kind of adrenalised aural ferality. Not in a benign, paternalistic way, or in any other philanthropy towards the benighted trained musician, that is sure. In standing where Beethoven and the banker stand, Cardew had the idea of the untrained musician in mind, and the graphic score of 'Paragraph 1' of *The Great Learning* at hand to set against that fermata. The preliminaries of 'Paragraph 1' have been discussed expertly and at length; the Chinese, calligraphic qualities of the 'Stones' Chorus' portion of it, especially so. In relation to Beethoven's authoritarian fermata, however, the significance of the marks made to describe the activity of the performance of the 'Stones' Chorus' seems specific in other ways. Here, Cardew hands over to the performers the interpretation of both the notation in the score and the actions of the conductor. This can be various. Eddie Prévost has related stories of rainy treks across northern landscapes in an unreliable van to secure supplies of appropriately musical pebbles for the performance of the Chorus section. Such stories have a vivid, anecdotal capacity to set in motion themes of refined technical skill, esoteric knowledge and questing, uncompromising camaraderie. This provides a kind of narrative time that is not asked for by the score, but not refused either. Yet it is only one kind of time. What other affects might be contained by the acoustic outlines of the pauses, hesitations, waitings, that prefigure the individual tapping of stones and the syncopated carapace that the ensuing tumbling sound produces, can only be guessed at from the outside. This is the point, because from the inside of the performance it might be possible to know all too well what minor history motivates the beauties of each act of interpretation and improvisation (within the constraints to which such symptoms may be trusted).

In the same ways as theories of relational aesthetics plague and overly anticipate the findings of contemporary art practices – and in the same ways that a second language of community, dispersal and mutation handicaps an engaged inquiry into the aesthetics of modern critical sociability – so too the experimental music community in Britain in the 1970s suffered with an attempt to explain it. Brilliant and perceptive in many ways, documenting and detailing a host of experiments in intersubjectivity, in fleetingness and ambiguity, Michael Nyman's book *Experimental Music* was written too early. At least, it feels as if the existence of this handbook to new musical perception blanketed something. To an extent, it reduced many things to sharp one-liners, and it may not have been incorrect in doing so. Cardew, himself no mean manual-writer, appears as a pivotal figure in the book, perhaps rightly so. Nyman's habit in that book is to make equations. This score corresponds to that subjective insight, whether it be a political one, an aesthetic or one to do with the character of time or chance. It may have to do with a soul-saturating attention to a sonority or a repetition. It may be to do with the denial of causal relationships between things, or the simple solving of a riddle. For Nyman's diagnostic manner, whatever the relationship between score and perceived outcome is suggested, the work appears as fully that. Contrarily, what is riveting throughout Cardew's scores and descriptions of proposed actions, is the absolute refusal to allow for a single reading, no matter how grave, profound or diapasonic. When Cardew asks untrained singers to try and squeeze the rhythmically challenging political prose of Hardial Bains into the corsets of a 19th-century boating song, the result was (and still is) a set of delicious and unpredictable excesses to play with, feint and

almost unseizable. There is no way of getting it right, either in performance or allegorical listening. Everything that arises musically, steps with great grace beyond its defined subject matter, moving into perception unregulated, rapidly and surprisingly. The best that can be hoped for, in fact the treasure of the process, are the grounds of a set of proposed aesthetic fidelities, which might become the basis of a contingent, interpersonal politics, or something broader – the discrete lovelinesses of the struggle to approach radicalism. When Cardew instructs that one rearrange the stones in a brook to retune it, or order some instruments comfortably about oneself, lay down, walk about, play, or not, there is always an awareness that none of these things need actually to be done. There is no compunction behind this cold managerial tone. You don't have to do what you are told in order to fully experience and appreciate what the work allows. These are constraints designed to produce relative subjective surpluses, purposefully useless ones.

This is the composition of Cardew, an explicit and curious appeal to invent powerful moments of social time and the customs and habits that might be countenanced by it, an appeal to wonder about glances and old-fashioned looks, to find vectors of renewed social order in the burbles that are natural to under-rehearsed communal speaking and in the exquisitely polished agonies of percussive conversations. Hearing things, wondering if they have been heard by others, wondering how they might mean and be recalled or preserved in their unfinished condition, these are his performances. Where Cardew's compositional practices seem to direct themselves, in the *Schooltime Compositions* as much as in his discussion of Mao's 1942 lectures at Yan'an, is not a curatorial attempt to give an authoritatively medicinal account of the forms of subjectivity imposed on one's consciousness by capitalist society. Rather, whilst being that too, they are also directed towards engineering opportunities to uncover immediate and unheralded social possibilities through the properly dismissible practice of naming unseen wild flowers – from there finding a future. It really is that optimistic.

Contents

The Great Learning, paragraph 1
2 pages
For chorus (speaking and playing whistles and stones) and organ.
Duration about 30 minutes
Composition dated 31.4.68

Content: WHAT THE GREAT LEARNING TEACHES IS — TO ILLUSTRATE ILLUSTRIOUS VIRTUE; TO RENOVATE THE PEOPLE; AND TO REST IN THE HIGHEST EXCELLENCE.

The Great Learning, paragraph 2
1 page
For singers and drummers.
Duration about 1 hour
Composition dated January 1969

Content: THE POINT WHERE TO REST BEING KNOWN, THE OBJECT OF PURSUIT IS THEN DETERMINED; AND THAT BEING DETERMINED, A CALM UNPERTURB-EDNESS MAY BE ATTAINED TO. TO THAT CALMNESS THERE WILL SUCCEED A TRANQUIL REPOSE. IN THAT REPOSE THERE MAY BE CAREFUL DELIBERATION, AND THAT DELIBERATION WILL BE FOLLOWED BY THE ATTAINMENT (OF THE DESIRED END).

The Great Learning, paragraph 3
1 page
For large instruments and voices
Duration about 45 minutes
Composition dated 14.7.70

Content: THINGS HAVE THEIR ROOT AND TH BRANCHES. AFFAIRS HAVE THEIR END AND T BEGINNING. TO KNOW WHAT IS FIRST AND WHA LAST WILL LEAD NEAR TO WHAT IS TAUGHT (IN GREAT LEARNING).

The Great Learning, paragraph 4
5 pages
For chorus (shouting and playing ridge notched instruments, sonorous substances rattles or jingles) and organ.
Duration about 40 minutes.
Composition dated 10.4.70

Content: THE ANCIENTS WHO WISHED TO ILLUSTRATE ILLUSTRIOUS VIRTUE THROUGHOUT KINGDOM, FIRST ORDERED WELL THEIR OWN STATES. WISHING TO ORDER WELL THEIR STAT THEY FIRST REGULATED THEIR FAMILIES. W TO REGULATE THEIR FAMILIES, THEY FIRST CULT THEIR PERSONS. WISHING TO CULTIVATE THEIR PERSONS, THEY FIRST RECTIFIED THEIR HEA WISHING TO RECTIFY THEIR HEARTS, THEY FIRS SOUGHT TO BE SINCERE IN THEIR THOUGHTS. W TO BE SINCERE IN THEIR THOUGHTS, THEY FIRST EXTENDED TO THE UTMOST THEIR KNOWLEDGE SUCH EXTENSION OF KNOWLEDGE LAY IN THE INVESTIGATION OF THINGS.

Great Learning, paragraph 5

pages

a large number of untrained musicians
stures, performing actions, speaking,
and playing a wide range of instruments,
nally, 10 singers singing 'Ode Machines'
y also be performed separately.

ation about 2 hours
posed 1969-70

tent: THINGS BEING INVESTIGATED, KNOW-
CAME COMPLETE. THEIR KNOWLEDGE
MPLETE, THEIR THOUGHTS WERE SINCERE.
OUGHTS BEING SINCERE, THEIR HEARTS
N RECTIFIED. THEIR HEARTS BEING RECT-
EIR PERSONS WERE CULTIVATED. THEIR
BEING CULTIVATED, THEIR FAMILIES WERE
D. THEIR FAMILIES BEING REGULATED, THEIR
ERE RIGHTLY GOVERNED. THEIR STATES
GHTLY GOVERNED, THE WHOLE KINGDOM
E TRANQUIL AND HAPPY.

Great Learning, paragraph 6

page

any number of untrained musicians
ation about 30 minutes
nposition dated October 1969

tent: FROM THE SON OF HEAVEN DOWN
MASS OF THE PEOPLE, ALL MUST CONSIDER
TIVATION OF THE PERSON THE ROOT (OF
NG BESIDES).

The Great Learning, paragraph 7

½ page

For any number of untrained voices
Duration about 90 minutes
Composition dated 8.4.69

Content: IT CANNOT BE, WHEN THE ROOT IS
NEGLECTED, THAT WHAT SHOULD SPRING FROM IT
WILL BE WELL ORDERED. IT NEVER HAS BEEN THE
CASE THAT WHAT WAS OF GREAT IMPORTANCE HAS
BEEN SLIGHTLY CARED FOR, AND, AT THE SAME TIME,
THAT WHAT WAS OF SLIGHT IMPORTANCE HAS BEEN
GREATLY CARED FOR.

Second printing. June 1971
Third printing. June 1984

1

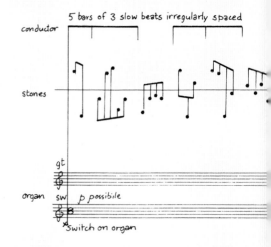

The Great Learning, paragraph 1

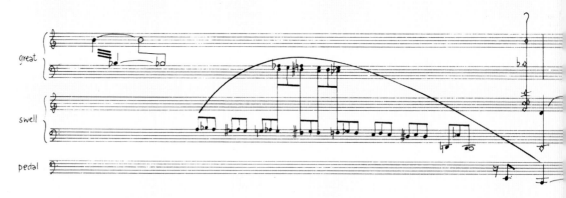

1.1

(G# if available)

with each note

Action Score

Sentence 1

SOFT
streamer
COINGAME
swoosh
drum
wand/IMAGE (shake)
sheet
light

streamer
COINGAME
LEGWORK
floor
drum
dumbshow/LIGHT
guero
handgame
swoosh/whistle
overhead

dumbshow
drum
ballgame
SWOOSH
coingame/whistle (walk)
handgame

FACE
heavy
coingame
swoosh/handgame
overhead/LOCOMOT

Sentence 2

SHAKE
cardgame
whistle
heavy — tool
SPIN
dumbshow
cardgame/skip
whistle

ballgame
WALK/cardgame
mouth
whistle
streamer
OVERHEAD

coingame
tool
swoosh
WHISTLE
heavy/swish (soft)
dumbshow

WALK/DRUM
handgame
heavy
whistle/dumbshow
swish

ballgame
coingame
locomotion
tool
CARDGAME
heavy
handgame/dum
whistle
overhead
drum
SHEET (guero)
face
swish

Sentence 3

overhead
swish
machine
soft
SWOOSH
handgame
heavy/coingame
streamer
dumbshow
light
RATTLE (stamp)
tool
guero

OVERHEAD
swish
swoosh
heavy
whistle
streamer/HANDGAME
skip
swoosh
cardgame — legwork
heavy/COINGAME (tool)
STONE (fall)
locomotion
shake

swish/ballgame (guero)
soft
whistle
STREAMER
handgame
coingame

VOICE
heavy
handgame
streamer/coingame
skip
LIGHT

Sentence 4

TOOL
locomotion — drum
mouth — floor
face

swish
STREAMER
handgame
skip
BALLGAME

overhead/swoosh
stone
skip
CARDGAME (locomotion)
dumbshow
heavy

MACHINE
guero
handgame
DUMBSHOW
cardgame/heavy
ballgame

rattle
DUMBSH
overhead
whistle
HANDGA
cardgam
drum —

5.3

(continuing from previous page)
SKIPPING ODE: If a performer takes up the option of singing this ode he is exempted from other responsibility (e.g. simultaneous actions, text recitations, etc) until such time as he has completed it.

whistle
FACE/streamer
GUERO

drum swoosh
cardgame
overhead

histle

1E

EAVY

— rattle
/DUMBSHOW (face)
fall)

ON THE MOUNTAIN STANDS A LA—DY WHO SHE IS I DO NOT KNOW

ALL SHE WANTS IS GOLD AND SIL—VER ALL SHE WANTS IS A NICE YOUNG MAN

ALL RIGHT .... (a girl's name) I'LL TELL YOUR MOTHER I SAW YOU KISSING

.... (a boy's name) ROUND THE CORNER. DO YOU LOVE HIM? (shouted)

(⌢ ⌢ ⌢) These could all be length-of-a-breath notes

YES NO YES NO .... Continue upward until no higher note can be sung. The last word is the answer. HOW MANY KISSES DID YOU GIVE HIM?

FIVE TEN FIFTEEN TWENTY.... WILL YOU MARRY HIM?

YES NO YES NO ....

Number Score (Interpretation)

overhead
CARDGAME
heavy
whistle
SKIP

RATTLE
dumbshow
STREAMER
tone
overhead
drum
FACE
heavy
andgame/swoosh (locomotion)
ardgame
oingame

MATRIX OF CATEGORIES										
I – social	II – scale	III – actions	IV – parts of the body	V – states	VI – ideas ("think about...")	VII – positions	VIII – objects	IX – materials	X – composition	
1 solo	huge	jump	foot	sleeping	Unity	to left	ball	wood	spun	1
2 duet	tiny	stamp	leg	waking	Multiplicity	to right	coin	metal	drawn	2
3 trio	big	swim/hop	fingers	anxiety	Birth	in front	card	stone	cast	3
4 quartet	small	shake	hand	expectancy	Rebirth/Reproduction	behind	rope/chain	earth/sand/clay/grit	constructed/knitted	4
5 quintet	generous	walk	arm	loving	Death	above	wand	glass	natural (raw)	5
6 large group	economical	float	shoulder	dreaming	Humanity	below	streamer	leather/skin	blown (hollow)	6
7 dissenting	mean	kick	hip	wonder	Nature	inside	tool	dust/gas	woven	7
8 leading	microscopic	spin	head	active	Good	outside	heavy object	plastic	carved	8
9 assisting	cosmic	crawl	mouth	still	Evil	horizontal	toy	water/oil/milk	juxtaposed	9
10 gregarious	swelling	run	teeth	wandering	Revolution	vertical	handkerchief	flesh	fused	10
11 passenger	shrinking	roll	tongue	randy	Permanence	off at an angle	light object	blood	fixed	11
12 misanthropic	middling	cartwheel/skip	hair	communicative	Transience	out of sight	musical instrument	rubber	loose	12

SUGGESTED METHOD OF INTERPRETATION: Take a 4-digit number (it could be derived from your birthdate), convert the digits into Roman numerals (O becomes X) and read off from the matrix of categories (above) four categories to be represented by the letters A, B, C, D in the score. The numbers in the score are then read as the corresponding items in these categories.

FOR EXAMPLE: 1840 (from the birthdate 1. August 1940) gives A = I, B = VIII, C = IV, D = X, and the beginning of sentence 1 of the Number Score thus produces the verbal matrix: leg, card, duet, wand. The interpretation and performance of this is entirely free. This is the freedom of the fortune-teller. No-one can expect you to justify your interpretation. Your interpretation is self-justifying. The example might produce the following performance: Strike a playing card with a wand. Slip the playing card into someone else's sock and the wand into your own.

A particular 4-digit number may be used in only one sentence of the score. If a player is involved in other sentences he must use new numbers. Anything in the matrix of categories may be changed – categories, items, order of items.

13

The Revolution Will (Not) Be Improvised

Andrea Phillips

> We are *searching* for sounds and for the responses that attach to them, rather than thinking them up, preparing them and producing them. The search is conducted in the medium of sound and the musician himself is at the heart of the experiment.
>
> Cornelius Cardew, 'Towards an Ethic of Improvisation' [1]

Recent returns to participation in the visual arts record, depending on your point of view, either an unfinished social project or one of the many ways in which creativity can be mobilised to governmentalise public behaviour. Cornelius Cardew's work acts as a precursor to this distinction between aspirations for political inclusivity and the supposition of their inevitable foreclosure. Cardew sought to practice music as a social project throughout his life, marginalising establishments and institutions as he endeavoured to alter distinctions between composer, musician and audience. As such, he leaves a difficult legacy, and one that is consistently fought over, as he is claimed by both those that believe music (and, by extension, art in general) is a popular, often localised and always socialising practice and those that believe that structural experimentation is the route to reconceptualising change.

In between composing *Treatise* (1963–7), joining the free improvisation group AMM (1966), forming the Scratch Orchestra (1969), developing his major work *The Great Learning* (1968–70), and labelling all of this activity bourgeois and therefore dismissible in the name of revolutionary politics, Cardew developed a devastatingly accurate description of improvisation as a form that both democratises the musical process, allowing the many to join the few, the professional to join the amateur, in massive and often startling performance, and as one that exacerbates the divisions of skill at stake in

the privilege of taking up such space in the first place. From his 1968 essay 'Towards an Ethic of Improvisation' to his denunciative publication of 1974, *Stockhausen Serves Imperialism*, Cardew's trajectory exemplifies an intellectual journey in which the internal logics of collectively produced spaces of freedom available to artists, musicians, writers, etc., are tested by the limitations of their claims for immanent and companionable change. If, as Virginia Anderson says of the period, 'the act of improvisation was one of shared ownership and responsibility, in which all members were creative equals', then questions of equality in improvisation were – are – consistently striated by the imperatives of expertise. [2]

There are clear comparisons between Cardew's approach to improvisation and a continuing tactic amongst contemporary artists to keep the space of improvisation 'open' – uncaught – in a bid to produce an aesthetic promise of indeterminacy. Improvisation is a recurring trope across generations of creative practitioners, from artists through curators, web designers, architects, producers – who seek to collectivise and democratise within a milieu whose dominant forces of production privilege spectacular and elite forms. Improvisation also emerges in other fields as an unremarked principle of production – in certain forms of political philosophy and sociology, in utopian urbanism and human geography, in both anti- and pro-globalisation debates as well as in alternative and collectivised forms of immediate activism. If there is a recurring politics of improvisation, a paradoxical framing of the potential of transitivity and spontaneity, then does it have any productive force?

Cardew's interest in improvisation began by all accounts as he worked through and beyond serialist composition whilst engaged as an apprentice to, and then collaborator with,

Karlheinz Stockhausen in Cologne in the late 1950s. Here, partly as a response to his growing critique of the strictures of Stockhausen's extremely regulated composition, Cardew saw that the concept of musical notation might shift from that of a set of strict instructions to be attended to by conductor and musician with utmost perspicacity to one in which notation became more gestural, stretched in its semantic potential, indicating not a legal framework for performance but instead a site of transitivity whereby a set of decisions might be understood as arbitrary, impulsive, context-specific, flexible. Writing on what became known as free improvisation in his extensive biography of Cardew, John Tilbury describes this early desire to produce an 'omnipresent, uncatchable, free music … free from the tyranny of baton and barline'.[3]

Ethics of Improvisation

It could be said that Cardew embraced and sought to exemplify improvisation as a form of 'live ethics' in various forms, from the beginning of his work on *Treatise* until the demise of the Scratch Orchestra in 1972. In these various forms improvisation provided a means not simply through which the traditionally hierarchical relationship between composer, conductor, players and audience was (reputedly) erased but through which the conceptual bounds of what constituted composition might be rethought. Inspired variously by his encounters with the work of John Cage and David Tudor, his growing awareness of inequality within the UK and elsewhere, and his work with AMM, the concept of improvisation provided Cardew, like many artists of this period, with a mode through which to share the formats of production, equalise concepts of creativity and eradicate boundaries and distinctions of skill, profession, position and

educational context. In addition, it allowed Cardew to recognise – and produce what might be termed approximations to – the idea of immanent or uncatchable, non-repeatable or reproducible creativity in forms that were, ostensibly, open to all. In 'Towards an Ethic of Improvisation', published in the *Treatise Handbook* in 1971, Cardew asks:

> [W]ho can be interested purely in sound, however high its 'fidelity'? Improvisation is a language spontaneously developed amongst the players and between players and listeners. Who can say in what consists the mode of operation of this language?[4]

Written whilst heavily immersed in AMM, and primarily influenced by the experience of playing with – rather than composing for – the group, in this essay Cardew asserts the belief in the chance encounter of sounds – everyday and from within the state of acknowledged musicality – as an ethical procedure through which indeterminacy produces a state that is at once dependent and independent, reliant and open to change. In improvisation,

> [t]wo things running concurrently in haphazard fashion suddenly synchronise autonomously and sling you *forcibly* into a new phase. Rather like in the 6-day cycle race when you sling your partner into the next lap with a forcible handclasp. Yes, improvisation is a sport *too*, and a spectator sport, where the subtlest interplay on the physical level can throw into high relief some of the mystery of being alive. Connected with this is the proposition that improvisation cannot be rehearsed. Training is substituted for rehearsal, and a certain moral discipline is an essential part of this training.[5]

Suggesting that the best people to produce such a search are 'musical innocents' who might develop the virtues of 'simplicity', 'integrity', 'selflessness', 'forbearance', 'preparedness' and 'identification with nature' in order to be receptive enough to improvise, Cardew concludes, 'From a certain point of view improvisation is the highest mode of musical activity, for it is based on the acceptance of music's fatal weakness and essential and most beautiful characteristic – its transience.'[6]

In retrospect, Cardew's written accompaniment to *Treatise* can be identified with a generalised sense of collective ethics, in which improvisation is described as a state of grace through which acceptance of life and its different sounds is a high achievement to be communicated intra-socially and disseminated pedagogically via participation in performances of variable dimensions and durations. As such it prefigures many artistic and philosophical attempts to identify and work outside hierarchically organised spaces. Cardew was influenced by time spent with choreographers and dancers attempting to achieve a similar state of immersion within a sensory time and space of what he terms transience, and he shared with his avant-garde predecessors the influence of Eastern philosophy upon his practice. Analogies can also be made to forms of phenomenology emerging from Europe in the early 1970s in which states of deterritorialisation run in a similar vein. This imperative is for Cardew also informed by a more pragmatic recognition of the politics of artistic (musical) production. John Tilbury quotes from Cardew's diary notes of 1967–8:

> Something about the strongest things being not commercially viable. Commercially viable in the age of technology means reproducible in unlimited numbers or broadcastable. A music that is local in inspiration is therefore not commercially viable.[7]

This investment in improvisation as a non-objectifying, non-commodifiable, collectivising and ethical process was shared by artists from a number of fields working in the late 1960s and early 1970s. Inspired by Beat and action poetry, Fluxus and Dada, the novels of William Burroughs, the concept of chance developed by Cage and Jackson Pollock's action painting, the choreographer-dancer Steve Paxton, a founder member of the Judson Church Dance Theater, developed Contact Improvisation, a physical parallel with free improvisation in which dancers would work under a number of loose rules to explore the 'physical forces imposed on the body by gravity, by the physics of momentum … made by the dancer in the moment of dancing'.[8] In her work *Three Distributions*, published in *Aspen* no.8 (edited by Dan Graham, himself a strong supporter of spontaneous production within popular music, published in Winter 1970/1), choreographer Yvonne Rainer instructs a group of professional and non-professional performers to move according to precise rules that establish, rather then deliberative improvisation, the 'volition' of the body in its collective state of grace: 'We occupy space, when one of us moves out of that space he leaves room for another to enter, or for an inanimate object to be placed there. This place is chock-full of redistributable material.'[9]

Allan Kaprow, describing the happening *Self Service* (1967) outlines a set of rules for a performance lasting four months in three American cities, as 'a piece without spectators' in which 31 actions are selected by the artist and distributed amongst the cities for performance: 'Activities took place among those of the participants' normal lives. These were not necessarily coordinated; it was by chance that some actions turned out to be similar in two or all of the cities.'[10] There are many similar examples.

Improvisation Rites

Within the 'Ethics' essay, there is still a reliance on concepts of training. Moral discipline, as Cardew puts it, is matched by the musician's ability to listen, concur with and allow for the performance of others (and with AMM, this becomes a carefully honed and finely tuned craft: watching AMM perform, one is constantly reminded of exactly how highly skilled these musicians are, exactly how much musical experience it takes to be able to engage in the micro-maturations of sound they assemble). The Scratch Orchestra, formed initially via Cardew's teaching at Morley College, can be seen as a test both to the intricate relations of AMM and to the broader conception of social transformation generalised within AMM's formula of improvisation. Here the testing ground for Cardew's politics emerges, as it does for improvisation. Can mass music-making produce the same indeterminacy exemplified in highly attuned situations created by the professional musicians of AMM, or does this call for another type of improvisation politics, in which exactitude is forgone in favour of participation?

Whilst in the early 1970s it was common within experimental music to accept the desire for what Virgina Anderson calls the 'increased equality of responsibility between composer and performer', Cardew's shift from *Treatise* and AMM to the Scratch Orchestra can be seen as a test of just how far this performance of equality – through the medium of free improvisation – might go. With no instructions whatsoever for the performer, *Treatise* already opened up the concept of 'indeterminacy', but was still harboured within the high modernist language of the avant-garde, despite and through its coincidence with AMM, its score a language of potentially arcane symbols and refined motivations. *Treatise* is mainly opaque to anyone without an explicit relationship with the development of scoring from Boulez, Ligeti, Nono, et al. But with the Scratch Orchestra, regulation took a different turn. No musical education was necessary to take a part in the orchestra, and its organisation directly reflected common experiments with collectivity emergent through this time. Anderson describes its milieu:

> The Scratch Orchestra, as with many groups of the late 1960s, attracted people who wanted to 'do their own thing'. While some members worked to perform large-scale works such as *The Great Learning*, others showed up and, say, crawled around the performing space dressed in Christmas-tree lights. This freedom eventually led to divisions among the members: musicians wanted to use their training, non-musicians wanted to retain text notation. Anarchic sub-groups wanted more freedom in musical performance, older members were tired of waiting for their chance to organise concerts, and most of the orchestra resented the common outside assumption that the Scratch Orchestra was Cardew's group.[11]

Here the political realities, as opposed to the ethical commitments, of improvisation become more apparent. Cardew at this time was shifting decisively towards forms of Marxist-Leninism that debarred the concepts of musical improvisation he had been working with for most of his professional life, a fact that rattled those who, equally but differently of the Left, wanted to embrace his vanguard waywardness as a composer. Working as a figure-head for the increasing dogmatisation of artistic-political relations, and producing a far stronger accompanying discourse to his musical output, based on a Marxist-Leninist analyses of the role of culture in revolutionary politics directly influenced by the teachings of Mao, Cardew came to embrace what is often described as a 'new tonality' in his work, returning to the popular Lieder and folk songs of the 19th century to produce works for what was hoped to be a broader audience. Coming to reject AMM as a model of elitist production, and through all this producing his major opus *The Great Learning* (1968–70), Cardew toiled to commensurate, and then rejected, a relation between long-held beliefs in the freedom of improvisation, and the dictates of Party imperatives regarding the revolutionary role of music in the transformation of society. *The Great Learning*, a work in seven 'Paragraphs' based on Ezra Pound's translation of Confucius's eponymous text, can be seen as a site of this transformation, partially written for, rather than in collaboration with the Scratch Orchestra and with Cardew very much at the helm, at times subscribing to old improvisatory values but also dominated by the imperative to enunciate a new unitary voice.

If improvisation in its utopian form is an ethical promise to the player (in that it proffers the potential of equality; of an aesthetics born of the desire for true democracy) then in performance it cannot be that for the listener. In *The Great Learning*, this becomes clear. As Confucius, via Pound, dictates the revolutionary capacity for music and creativity to collectivise the populus to serve the greater good of Maoism, so the intonation of a contradiction becomes apparent. Between dictate and freedom, performers of this nine-hour opus are given liberty to improvise but under the strictures of a mastery learned from the academy: beats are on time; cohabiting instruments (whether they be stones, pillows, toy whistles or oboes) give way to each other with polite accommodation. The tension here is between lightness of touch and flexibility as ethically charged subjectivities and as axiomatic instrumentalisations (Alain Badiou's

concept of fidelity springs to mind). Anyone who has improvised knows the difficulty of this tension: the reason why jazz has the unmeasured and ego-driven gap of the solo lies in this tension, too. Anyone who has heard *The Great Learning* will understand the blocked or exclusionary situatedness of the listener, whose role is extraneous in many ways to the capacity of the work.

Improvisation Rights

In 1989, [Gavin Bryars's] *The Sinking of the Titanic* and *Jesus' Blood Never Failed Me Yet* were re-recorded, the latter with a performance by Tom Waits replacing the original documentary tape-loop. This substitution was indicative: a camera-ready Hollywood celebrity replaced an upsetting document of penury. *The Sinking of the Titanic* itself became a harmless montage of sound effects. Clean recording deprived it of the disquieting mournfulness of its first recording; the strings were 'well-played'. In reviews, no one referenced the original, just as no one remembered the intense debates about composition and improvisation – and revolution – that had surrounded it. Cornelius Cardew's Scratch Orchestra, whose manifestations Bryars took part in, had promised to bring down all the divisions and hierarchies of capitalism. Gavin Bryars's Portsmouth Sinfonia may have lacked such political ambitions, but it still translated amateur performance into something provocative and satirical ... However by the late 1990s, with Gavin Bryars writing a requiem for performance at Westminster Abbey – Tony Blair in attendance – and Michael Nyman wrecking the political thrust of David King's Trotskyist photo-essay *The Commissar Vanishes* at The Barbican, it was revealed that the political radicalism of the 1970s was simply the noise of artists courting the attention of the establishment.[12]

Improvisation occurs as an aesthetic device in many contemporary artists' work and, of course, is a viable and tested method of production that has eased itself into the affective modes of culture on a general level. Now it is not difficult to understand that artists improvise (indeed they are taught to do so in art college), that curators improvise, that choreographers improvise, that chefs improvise, that footballers improvise, that philosophers improvise, and certainly that politicians improvise when put on the spot. The improvisation 'rites' established by the Scratch Orchestra as methods of initiation give way to *rights* to improvisation, whereby the demand for uncommodified and non-descriptive space and time within culture takes on a different air. Whilst artists as diverse as Paul McCarthy, Iza Genzken, Dominique Gonzalez-Foerster, Ryan Gander, Josephine Meckseper, Wade Guyton or Jonathan Monk, in different ways, might stage improvisation on film or in the gallery as a conceptual and/or methodological device, there is in this aestheticisation a playing out of the difference between paradoxical (or ambivalent) staging and committed choice-making. Other practices are more forceful in their attempted actualisations of improvisation in action. Collectives like Ultra-red, for example, renew a call for improvisation on very different terms. Asking how the processes of organising might be understood as the formal practices that 'build relationships out of which people compose an analysis and strategic actions', they develop workshops, performances and collective actions that reverse the institutional tendency to understand politics in art as primarily related to a work's content.[13] Instead Ultra-red, whose outputs are variously to be found in galleries, protest groups and other political activist sites, propose a relation between participation, sound, subjectivity and emancipation at the level of structural change. Through Ultra-red, it is possible to understand another mechanism at work in the legacy of Cardew that has nothing to do with music but everything to do with composition (and here Jacques Rancière's work on the relation between equality and the aesthetics of sensible distribution becomes highly relevant). Cardew knew, certainly by the end of his foreshortened life, that politics is social composition and, as such, improvisation is both necessary and simply not enough.

To claim political rights for improvisation, therefore, is to tread a thin line between one form of emancipatory communitarianism and another form of liberalism. Here, the paradoxical formatting of much contemporary political work is revealed as a problem in so far as the ossification of politics occurs in new forms through the constellation of options, the recognition of contradictions, the consensualisation of oppositions occurring in repeatedly aestheticised forms. In recognition of this, the Micropolitics Research Group – based at Goldsmiths, University of London, and made up of artists, curators and theorists – asks, 'How can artists begin to distinguish, let alone imagine a practice that does not merely feed and replicate the machine itself? How can art practices that in Suely Rolnik's words bring "mutations of the sensible" into the realm of the visible or speakable, refuse or exit the limited field of possibility inscribed by late capitalism?'[14] So too, Chto delat, a collective of artists, curators and critics based in Petersburg, which publishes a regular newspaper that aims to 'merge' political theory, art and activism, usually in coincidence with an art project, exhibition or conference that they have organised or been asked to participate within. Inspired by the 'art soviets' set up in the USSR after the revolution, Chto delat (Lenin's 'What is to be done?') sees itself as a 'self-organising platform for cultural workers intent on politicising their "knowledge production" through reflections and redefinitions of an engaged autonomy for cultural practice today'.[15] If Ultra-red, the Micropolitics Research Group and Chto delat can be seen to continue a line of inquiry in which the necessity to produce an 'engaged culture' results in forms of direct action by artists and their collaborators, they stand as an alternative to the paradoxical ambivalence supported keenly by dominant curatorial and institutional tastes, even as they lend themselves to and gain notoriety through this same system.

> The community of equals can always be realised, but only on two conditions. First, it is not a goal to be reached but a supposition to be posited from the outset and endlessly reposited … The second condition, which is much like the first, may be expressed as follows: the community of equals can never achieve substantial form as a social institution. It is tied to the act of its own verification, which is forever in need of reiteration. No matter how many individuals become emancipated, society can never be emancipated.[16]

Between a necessity to 'endlessly reposit' equality and the insistence that creative production might have a substantiated relation to the distribution of the sensible, lie the forms of improvisation that Cardew initiated, committed to, questioned, rejected. Contemporary questions concerning the nature of political change within the cultures of immaterial labour and constelled subjectivities complicate the pragmatisim with which Cardew turned to Marxist-Leninism to find a blueprint for relations between art and politics. But his work stands as a test to aestheticisations of the paradoxical kind. Indeterminacies and transitivities appear and reappear, engage and disengage across decades. At stake is the revolutionary potential of improvisation – as a right not a rite – through which artists, musicians, curators and citizens might not simply inhabit the spaces left to them in the name of cultural production for spontaneous action, but insist on their expansion.

1   Cornelius Cardew, 'Towards an Ethic of Improvisation', 1968, anthologised in his *Treatise Handbook* (London: Edition Peters, 1971), available at www.ubu.com/papers/cardew_ethics.html.

2   Virginia Anderson, 'Cornelius Cardew Lives', Open Democracy News Analysis, 13 December 2007 (www.opendemocracy.net).

3   John Tilbury, *Cornelius Cardew (1936–1981): A Life Unfinished* (Harlow, UK: Copula, 2008), p.285.

4   Ibid.

5   Ibid.

6   Ibid.

7   Cornelius Cardew, quoted in ibid., p.352.

8   See www.touchdowndance.co.uk/graphic/contact_improvisation.html.

9   See www.ubu.com/aspen/aspen8/index.html and follow the link to section 8.

10 Allan Kaprow quoted in Mariellen R. Sandford (ed.), *Happenings and Other Acts* (London: Routledge, 1995), p.230.

11 Virginia Anderson, 'Cornelius Cardew Lives'.

12 Ben Watson, *Derek Bailey and the Story of Free Improvisation* (London: Verso, 2004), p.131.

13 Ultra Red, www.ultrared.org.

14 Micropolitics Research Group, http://micropolitics.wordpress.com.

15 Chto delat, www.chtodelat.org.

16 Jacques Rancière, *On the Shores of Politics* (London: Verso, 1995), p.84.

What is the experiment?

Central Institute for Nationalities.

With a whole team we are going to try ...

In what field?

215
9-6

A Discussion Meeting.

Acting, for example...

Theatre ?

Indian women's delegation in the USSR,
Leningrad, June, 1953.

46. Members of the delegation by
the Big Water-works in Petrodvorets
(Peter's Palace), Leningrad region.

Photo by A. Mikhailov and N. Nasomenkov.

Yes in a theatre in Chalon.
The Bourgogne Theatre we will try to...

You are moving to the provinces?

Begrüßung der ausländischen Delegierten auf
dem 4. Mütterkongress in Tokio
Von l. nach r.
Mrs. Ghyanchang   JJFF, Indien
Helga Dobel   JJFF, Westdeutschland
India
Mrs. Soemardjo, Mütterbewegung gegen A + H Bomben
Indonesien

Yes I will move to Bourgogne.
But you know, Chalon is not so far.

Don't you find it sad to leave Paris?

JAPAN PRESS
3—30 Shiba-Shinbashi,
Minato-ku, Tokyo, Japan.

No, I am glad.

You are pleased?

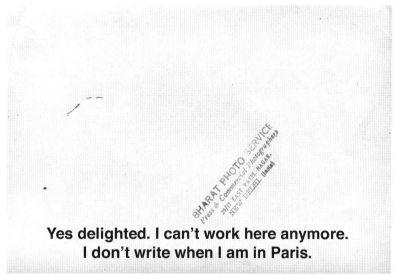

**Yes delighted. I can't work here anymore.
I don't write when I am in Paris.**

I am not making any progress here with my books.
Maybe when I start this experiment
I will do some writing as well.

Is it important to carry out an action?

Indian women's delegation in the USSR,
Sochy, July, 1953.

82. Members of the delegation visiting the Sochy Dendrarium.

Photo E. Shoolepov.

Yes, if it can be effective.
I don't want to start something for fun
or to soothe my conscience.

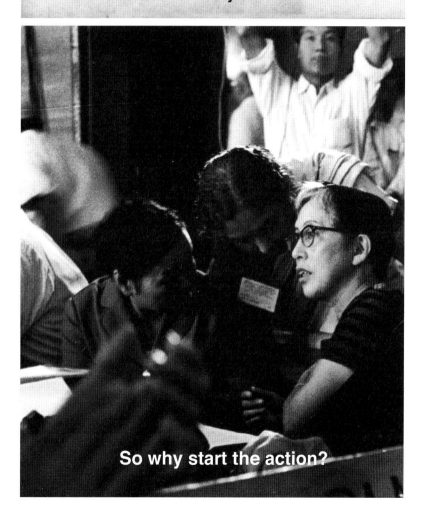

So why start the action?

Indian women's delegation in the USSR. Tashkent City, July 1953.

108. City women's meeting in the Navoi theatre. Vassilia Sadykova, member of the Soviet delegation, reporting to the Uzbek women on the results and decisions of the Women's World Congress held in Copenhagen on June 5-11 1953.

Photo by L. Danilov.

**It seems to me that something can be done
to place today's men and women
in a position to receive the world as it is...**

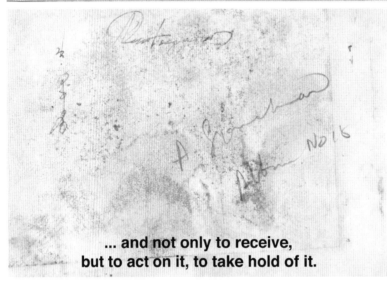

**... and not only to receive,
but to act on it, to take hold of it.**

Does that mean you are leaving the university?

If that is how you see it, then yes, I am leaving behind an attitude that is widespread in the university.

4

**The attitude of regarding the others,
those we address as receivers
purely and simply. It is the truth, I wouldn't want to be..**

3

**But Francis, don't you think
what is happening in China is important?**

In *Communists Like Us*, Anjalika Sagar and Kodwo Eshun spin a rich historical web prompted by a voyage taken by Sagar's grandmother to Mao's China. The Group present elements from its universe of materials configured in the form of a hypothetical 30-minute trailer for a new film in development. Photographs of the journey are transposed with subtitles from Godard's 1967 film *La Chinoise*. The resulting essay is a transcultural exchange that intertwines the postcolonial and the postmodern. The Otolith Group explores the potentiality of a 16-minute scene from *La Chinoise* which is filmed as an uninterrupted train journey. The indexical figure of activist turned philosopher Francis Jeanson argues with the fictional character of Véronique, a young Maoist student, played by Anne Wiasemsky. The dialogue from the scene has been transcribed onto the recto and the verso of archival photographs, thereby creating a contrapuntal conversation between photography and cinema. At the same time, different moments from the discrepant engagements with Maoism were brought into dialogue with each other. This differential reception was complicated by the projection of propaganda posters from the Cultural Revolution and the replaying of 'Paragraph 2' of *The Great Learning* composed by Cornelius Cardew in 1969 and performed by the Scratch Orchestra. Cardew's composition was chosen for the ways in which it enacts a practice of radical democracy through collective musical practice while simultaneously being a meditation on Confucian ethics. The resulting presentation brought the different moments from the discrepant engagements with Maoism into dialogue with each other.

Preliminary notes on *The Cardew Object* to be presented on the occasion of the symposium *Play for Today: Cornelius Cardew* at the ICA, London, 21 and 22 November 2009, the 40th Anniversary (plus seven months) of the ten-hour *Schooltime Compositions* performance at the ICA.
Prepared by Ultra-red, with contributions from Nelly Alfandari, William Crisp, Lucie Galand, Andrea Giulivi, Chris Jones, Fozia Khaliq, Anna Kontopoulou, Robbie Lockwood and Rashmi Munikempanna for discussion, revision, dissemination and practice.

Schooltime Compositions marks a key moment in Cornelius Cardew's transition from the classroom as privileged site of music pedagogy to that of the more phenomenological space of embodying the sound that would become *The Great Learning.* Perhaps due to its more benign character, it is a transition that generally receives less attention than the more incendiary move into Cardew's later period of composing music as a member of the Communist Party of England (Marxist-Leninist) and, from 1979 until his death, the Revolutionary Communist Party of Britain (Marxist-Leninist). In the case of his later transition, terms like 'cut' and 'rupture' figure in most commentaries of Cardew's move from the aesthetic to the political avant-garde. However, as we have learned from critiques of other attempts to mark epistemological breaks in the field of Marxism, an over-zealous attention *ex post facto* on transition as break has the all-too-common tendency of occluding those structural concerns that situate shifts within a persistent problematic. Going by titles alone, we can begin to identify just such a problematic as that of pedagogy – how is composition schooled and learned? Whether one's beacon is Cage or Mao, the relationships between composition and listening, teaching and learning, draw on the problematic of pedagogy.

It is not for merely superficial resemblances that Ultra-red turn from our own *School of Echoes* to a consideration of Cardew on the occasion of the 40th anniversary of the ten-hour performance of *Schooltime Compositions* at the ICA in London.[1] Aside from (or inside of) the aforementioned problematic, entering into such a reflection raises the potentials and the pitfalls of recollection, repetition and reconstruction that accompany learning the score. The easy way out, of course, is to attend to the drama as a substitution for the more difficult work of analysis. In the ongoing work to institutionalise Cardew, there has been no shortage of drama. As a preliminary note on our own investigation, this text functions more as a series of propositions than a foregone conclusion.

Perhaps Cardew lends himself to investigation for the simple fact that the project of institutionalisation itself remains unresolved. This is not to argue against such a project but, rather, to invite some clarity on the investments driving that endeavour. Any institution is bound to a series of investments. In his recent *Twenty Theses on Politics*, the Marxist political philosopher Enrique Dussel discusses how institutions become necessary for practice to be translated from one context to another.[2] Otherwise, the *we* and our way of organising ourselves can never outlive the purely improvisational moment. Far from empowering, remaining within the purely improvisational defeats our capacity to organise across political, cultural, linguistic and geographic conditions. It is the foreclosure of knowledge itself. To valorise such a foreclosure abandons us to a bitter lament of the inevitability of institutions. Conversely, to elevate the institution to a force of nature severed from investment places the power of the institution over the potentiality of its terms. There have been so many anthems blasted from loudspeakers on behalf of that kind of divinely ordained power. Lament or anthem, the noise fades, and we awaken to either a sense of defeat or triumph, unclear how it all happened. Might other sounds be possible? It is, if anything, the lesson of improvisation itself in which the cause of our listening has the status of an object – an object cause of the desire to listen and to train our ears. However, the organising of listening is not synonymous with analysis.

Now we have the invention of the institution of Cornelius Cardew, whose relation to the larger conceptualist moment remains on trial.[3] Perhaps part of those deliberations stems from open wounds that persist even decades after Cardew's death. Witness the May 2006 70th anniversary of Cardew at Cecil Sharpe House in London, where combating participants performed the competition between terms of a modernist avant-garde and a political avant-garde. At the July 2009 forum hosted by The Drawing Room, debates over improvisation versus structure became code for all-too-familiar aesthetic-political tensions. Characterised as a clash between ideological camps, this debate-that-refuses-resolution demands to be problematised and not simply resolved or abandoned.

As much can be learned from what the aesthetic/political avant-garde debate conceals as from what it reveals. On the one hand, it would be worth probing deeper how the division makes opaque the political investments of a modernist avant-garde position whether political or aesthetic. Given the collapse of hegemony around either avant-garde, it appears to be beside the point to aestheticise (or to politicise, for that matter) the Cardew institution. The greater urgency asks us to discover the terms of our own stake in listening to and attending to Cardew, and to see Cardew as a problem rather than as a surface. In the rush to enter Cardew into the canon – and which episodes of his oeuvre become canonised

have deep implications for an analysis of both the aesthetic-political and the political-aesthetic – Cardew becomes the means by which we can investigate the stakes in historicising or effacing altogether his politics, or his aesthetics, for that matter. Yet, even this inquiry only scratches the surface.

In his biography, *Cornelius Cardew (1936–1981): A Life Unfinished*, John Tilbury describes Cardew's militancy of the latter period as unoriginal and moralistic. At one point, Tilbury contrasts Cardew's unpleasant and naive iconoclasm with the 'humanity' of Bertolt Brecht and Hanns Eisler.[4] While Cardew's tone may certainly have differed in tone from that of Brecht and Eisler and his actions may have lacked their nuanced dialectical thinking, it is important to acknowledge why Cardew in his historical moment could never be Brecht; how it was that in the wake of postcolonial struggles, anti-imperialism brought about deep changes in the very institutions of the international Communist movement and how those changes would have a profound impact on an understanding of the aesthetic-political problematic. Over the course of decades marked by constant disillusionment with actually existing Communism combined with growing solidarity between revolutionary movements on the periphery and the children of empire, for Cardew and his contemporaries the role of the artist seemed far less Brechtian. But did their understanding of the artist's role still adhere to the modernist notion of the artist as, in Walter Benjamin's words, 'ideological patron' – artist as singularly the composer and/or distributor of the correct analysis?[5]

It is crucial to remember that even within the international revolutionary milieu there existed profoundly different ideas about the function and practice of culture. While some Communists saw culture purely instrumentally, in the postcolonial projects of Frantz Fanon and Paulo Freire, as well as many radical feminist communities, revolutionary education became a process of constituting critical collectivity and not merely a politically-correct content to be inscribed upon the surface of minds otherwise immersed in false consciousness. Debates around precisely this question often became the measure of one's conformity to or exclusion from the Party. Cardew's own surrender to the will of the Party, rather than resolving the political-aesthetic problematic, threw it into relief. We might characterise this as a crisis of listening or, rather, the limits of listening. After all, it is not as if Cardew feared that listening produces an unproductive repetition. Repetition is highly productive. People make careers out of just such a repetition. However, that which is repeated and produced may be neither transformative nor revolutionary. Seeing the need for something outside the composition, Cardew turned to a very specific, one could even say narrow, Maoist discourse and procedure.[6] With the benefit of hindsight, we may ascertain the limits of such a turn. However, we still find ourselves in a similar problematic. If listening and its procedures are seen as the antidote to the artist as 'ideological patron', then in the relationship between organising and pedagogy, what is the function of ideology in constructing the institutions of that practice? In other words, is it merely enough that we listen but that we assume responsibility for our practices of listening and the procedures by which we prepare ourselves to listen? The organisation of listening that, in a post-Cage world, is the function of the composition, is not equivalent to analysis, nor does it exhaust the need to study history, to teach each other and to build political literacy.

What, then, becomes possible when we pose as a question Cardew's later position on the artist's relationship to struggle and his subjection to the Party? As a problematic, the position asks, how might we hystericise this notion of the artist: Am I the author of the (com)position? Along these lines, we can visit anew the problem that dogged Cardew in both his aesthetic avant-garde and People's Liberation Music periods. What is a radical sound? What is the sound of the political? Or, more precisely: what will we have heard when we *hear* the political? What assumptions do we make about a political sound's proximity to, or distance from, identity or counter-identity, to the aesthetic? How does our status as composers of sound (and/or authors of analysis) change as a result of this line of inquiry? Does the political sound exist *in its composing* or is it in asking the question: 'What is the sound of the political?' Is it, in other words, *in the listening*? How do we organise that kind of listening? And does the organisation of listening exhaust the aesthetic-political problematic in the field of sound?

Through these questions, we begin to get at the fundamental issue of putting Cardew into play, to clarify what potentiality Cardew the institution makes possible within aesthetic and political improvisation. Hence we arrive at a series of propositions that arise out of Ultra-red's own investments in *The Cardew Object*. Some of these propositions are directed explicitly to Cardew and his oeuvre. Other propositions speak to a desire with only tangential parallels to Cardew. Both type of propositions become necessary for putting the researcher and the researched into process.

1. In his shift from the aesthetic avant-garde to the political avant-garde, and within assumptions about the undialectical incommensurability of those two positions (their unproblematic relation, if you will), Cardew's status as the author of the composition, the 'ideological patron', remains unchanged.

2. If composition, like any signifying practice, puts the subject into process, then over the course of his life, Cardew's own status as a movement artist, its composer, its patron, became increasingly tested. Such a test makes the contradiction of composition apparent: process versus position. One either problematises that contradiction, hears it as a threshold towards a potentiality (an 'untested feasibility', in Freire's words), or one retreats and shores up the authority of one's position exclusive of process.[7]

3. While we do not have Cardew himself to whom to direct our questions, we do have the record in the form of scores, recordings of performances, writings, and the memory of those who directly experienced the improvisational moment. Listening to the record for the sound of the political can recast the contradiction as a problematic provoking a response, a collective organisation of listening where the sound object no longer delivers an analysis but invites us as listeners to the problematic of process versus position.

4. In organised listening, we enter into process on our way towards an analysis.

5. What analysis might we (with whom?) strategically test in action?

We begin with the sound object – *The Cardew Object* – and then we ask: 'What did you hear?'

Over our 15 years of collective activities, Ultra-red has conducted numerous sound-based investigations into the political conditions of the AIDS crisis, social housing, anti-racism and the struggles of migration. Those investigations have been facilitated through protocols of field recording, public dialogue, organised listening, and *musique concrète*

composition. The formal procedures Ultra-red employs incorporate lessons from a range of radical traditions, including Freire's thematic investigation, popular education, militant inquiry and others.

The proposed project marks a unique departure for Ultra-red. Rather than entering into the aesthetic through political inquiry, *The Cardew Object* gives the collective access to the political through an explicitly aesthetic inquiry: the music of Cornelius Cardew. The project will unfold over the course of two phases: first, a rehearsal phase of four sessions and, second, a ten-hour performance to be presented during the *Play for Today: Cornelius Cardew* symposium at the ICA. For *The Cardew Object*, Ultra-red reunites with participants from the London sessions of the *School of Echoes* project. The analytical, pedagogical and artistic resonances between this collective and the collectives convened by Cardew 40 years prior, become the occasion for Ultra-red's engagement with Cardew in *The Cardew Object*. Additionally, in the space of transmitting procedures of listening to others, Ultra-red has become keenly aware of those potentials and the pitfalls that arise with the institutionalisation of a practice. For these reasons, Ultra-red invited members of the *School of Echoes* in London to join us in realising this inquiry – an inquiry whose form and content begins with the problem of the pedagogy of the ear.

When Ultra-red approached the participants in London's *School of Echoes* with the possibility of taking part in a performative investigation of Cornelius Cardew, we wanted to hear about the investments they would bring to such an inquiry. We asked the nine people who responded to the invitation to each write a statement about that investment. In their responses, all of them said that a major reason for joining the project was to continue with the work begun during the Raven Row Sessions of the *School of Echoes* project. With their various backgrounds as visual artists, musicians, activists, curators, teachers and students, the participants were eager to either continue the specific projects that emerged out of the sessions or to continue learning with Ultra-red. Others spoke more concretely about what was at stake for them in joining *The Cardew Object*. For several, the inquiry begins from a desire to resist an art world that can only accommodate site-specificity within the conditions of one site after another. In commuting a practice across serial contexts, the artist finds herself within the very contradiction of improvisation and institutionalisation mentioned at the beginning of this text. The very 'longing for connections' that an artist may identify as central to her work partly arises out of a desire to resist those conditions where 'residency' means the opposite.

The link between the questions of aesthetic and social organisation echoed in other statements. For one *School of Echoes* member, the aesthetic practice of listening disturbs the everyday life experiences of being attentive to the city. 'I have been listening, and I am getting undone by that listening,' she wrote. 'The loudness of racism, class, and citizenship that I meander through is extremely difficult. These are not projects I am involved with as an artist or activist. This is my life as it is lived in London.' Aware of her own resistance to the subject/object split, this member talked about being particularly mindful of what is meant by participation in art and its institutional contexts. She insisted that key questions like 'Who is allowed to speak, and what does that speaking then do to them?' should be first and foremost in any collective investigation. 'For me,' she concluded, 'who speaks and who listens are still extremely compartmentalised.'

Another *School of Echoes* member commented on the contradiction of the individual versus the collective as a consistent theme in Cardew's work. Along these lines, one of the more generous features of the early work of the Scratch Orchestra was the way in which it attempted to resolve this contradiction through an organised practice of confusion. Perhaps this is part of the appeal for many who come to inhabit Cardew's aesthetic avant-garde period. It is in the dislocation of certainty that entry-points are offered to the untrained musician – an enthusiasm for which was expressed by several *School of Echoes* members. For others, the terms of the aesthetic avant-garde hold deep resonance for the practice of politics in general. Here, the terms of 'improvisation, listening, pedagogy' – all features of Cardew's aesthetic avant-garde period – characterise other practices of political education such as Augusto Boal's Theatre of the Oppressed. One *School of Echoes* member discussed those same terms in relation to his years of activism: 'Thirty years of figuring out anarchist organising often seems like a durational performance that takes in composition, improvisation and the resultant incomprehension from others.'

But, to what extent does Cardew's praxis of improvisation, listening and pedagogy, together with problematics such as individual/collective and aesthetic/political avant-gardes function as anything more than historicised (and thereby irrelevant) terms? Or, as one *School of Echoes* member put it: 'What can we do with all of this?' It is a question that demands a different approach to *The Cardew Object* than one that seeks to merely enter Cardew into the canon – a project Cardew himself problematises in numerous ways.

Over the course of four rehearsal sessions, Ultra-red and our co-researchers from the *School of Echoes* will meet to establish a set of terms for engaging the work of Cardew. These terms will cover a range of issues as well as, potentially, a number of compositions and take the form of an analysis of scores and writings, collective listening to recordings, and other parallel research. The final outcome of the rehearsal sessions will be a protocol for organising the ten-hour performance to be presented at the ICA.

For the entire length of the ICA symposium (five hours each day), the members of Ultra-red along with members of the *School of Echoes* will publicly enact their research. The form of these enactments will be determined by the protocols designed during the rehearsal sessions. The entire performance will be open to the public who will be invited to contribute. The final outcome will be the articulation and analysis of, as well as proposals stemming from, new terms for further collective engagement into Cardew as an object cause of inquiry and collectivity.

1   *School of Echoes* was organised by Ultra-red during its residency at the London art centre Raven Row in spring 2009. The ten-week residency was accompanied by a five-session workshop on the practice of sound art and organising with 16 participants, among them, artists, activists, musicians, students, curators and political organisers.

2   Dussel argues that the relationship between popular struggle and its institutions must be founded on an 'obediential power' wherein institutions (including revolutionary political parties) must enact a practice of 'knowing how to listen to the other', rather than demanding obedience from below. Once institutions begin to adopt the latter, they move into a coercive relationship to popular struggles. Given their relationship to moments of social crisis, all artistic and cultural movements operate along the same power lines. Their institutions carry similar potentialities and the same risks. Enrique Dussel, *Twenty Theses on Politics*, tr. George Ciccariello-Maher (Durham, NC: Duke University Press, 2008), pp.24–9, 140 (n.17).

3   Here we are referring to the first generation of conceptual artists who either attended or felt the impact of Cage's Experimental Composition course at The New School for Social Research (1956–61); artists like George Brecht, Henry Flynt, George Maciunas, Yoko Ono and La Monte Young. In addition to having a personal acquaintance, Cardew promoted Young's music extensively throughout the 1960s. Cardew also spent time in the New York milieu during his 1966 residency at the Center of Creative and Performing Arts at State University of New York, Buffalo. The link begs a much larger art historical and critical question about the role of the sound arts in the development of conceptual art.

4   John Tilbury, *Cornelius Cardew (1936–1981): A Life Unfinished* (Harlow, UK: Copula, 2008), p.661. For Tilbury's analysis of Cardew's relationship to the work and politics of Brecht and Eisler, see Chapter 18, 'A Revolutionary Learning Curve 1975', pp.771–800.

5   Walter Benjamin, 'The Author as Producer' (1934), in Peter Demetz (ed.), *Reflections: Essays, Aphorisms, Autobiographical Writings* (New York: Schocken Books, 1986), p.228.

6   That is, until 1979, when mounting criticism of Mao's government precipitated a renunciation of Maoism and a subsequent turn to Enver Hoxha of Albania.

7   Defined by Freire as 'the future which we have yet to create by transforming today, the present reality. It is something not yet here but a potential, something beyond the "limit-situation" we face now, which must be created by us beyond the limits we discover.' Ira Shor and Paulo Freire, *A Pedagogy for Liberation: Dialogues on Transforming Education* (New York: Bergin & Garvey, 1987), p.153.

SCHOOLTIME
Compositions

Name _C. Cardew_

Year _1967_

Grade _480_

10/-

Schooltime Compositions

This 'Opera Book' was commissioned by Michael Sargent of
Focus Opera Group, and the first performance took place at
International Students House, London, on 11th and 12th
March 1968 under the titles Dayschool and Nightschool. The
individual compositions were interpreted simultaneously by the
composer, Lou Gare, Ranulf Glanville, Diana Gravill, Robin
Page, John David Pitchford of Dunstable, Keith Rowe, John
Tilbury, Christian Wolff, Bob Woolford and a chorus
assembled by Michael Graubart. 'Making A' was not
interpreted.

   Supplementary material is provided in an appendix.

All rights reserved

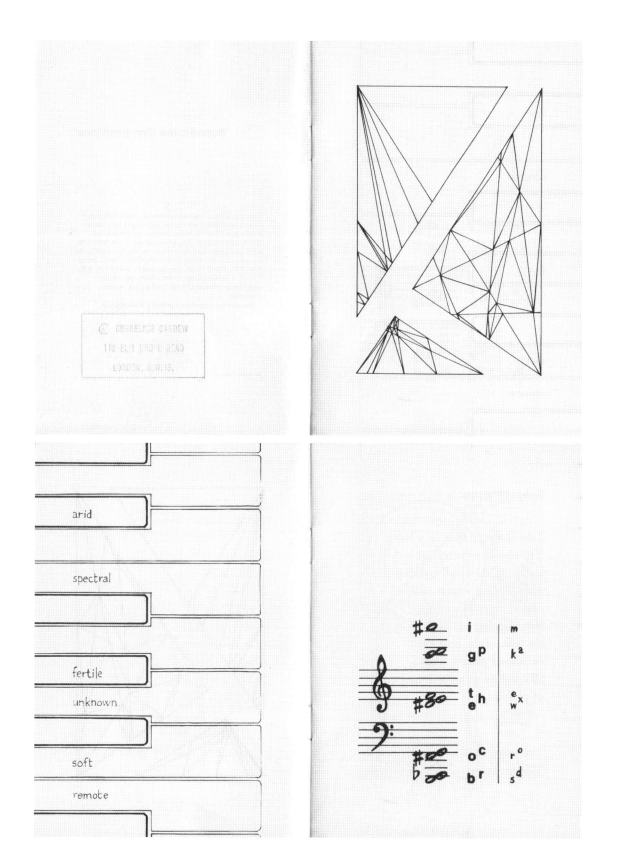

© CORNELIUS CARDEW
112 ELM GROVE ROAD
LONDON, S.W.13.

arid

spectral

fertile

unknown

soft

remote

Song of Pleasure

I am rowing a boat on a lake.
The sounds – the regular
breathing, the small creaking
and thudding sounds of the
oars in the rowlocks, the
water lapping and sucking at
the belly of the boat, the
occasional passing bird—
all combine to make a song
of pleasure.

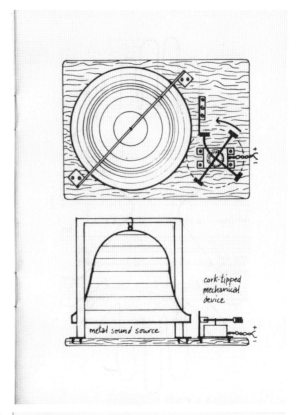

cork-tipped
mechanical
device

metal sound source

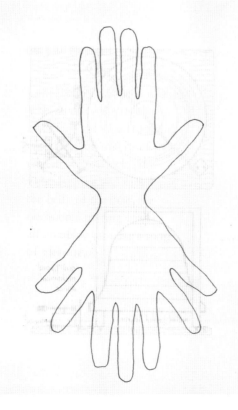

Vocals

tree
tri

you
i → ə → ɔ → o → u → x (a kiss)

me
m → ə → i   teeth bared;
lips pulled
right back

mother
m → ə → a — th(ə) → ə

scale: length of a breath

Melody

If the *ossia* is used,
the second and penultimate notes
of the mode should be omitted.

Making A

When A in the A-gauge glass becomes level with white line, make more A as follows:
1. Place WET B in glass bamer.
2. Empty one pack of A into the wet B.
3. Draw off two full measures of hot boiling C and pour them over the dry A in the B (using circular motion).
4. Draw off one FULL measure of A and repour it into B.
5. Close B between pours.
6. Never make more A if the A in A-gauge glass is above white line.

Every noise has a note

Desire

Want to do something; Do it

Do something without wanting to

Do something wanting not to

Be done to

Be done

note 1: Perform all or none of the instructions
note 2: Instructions are to be followed only by qualified person

Little flower of the North

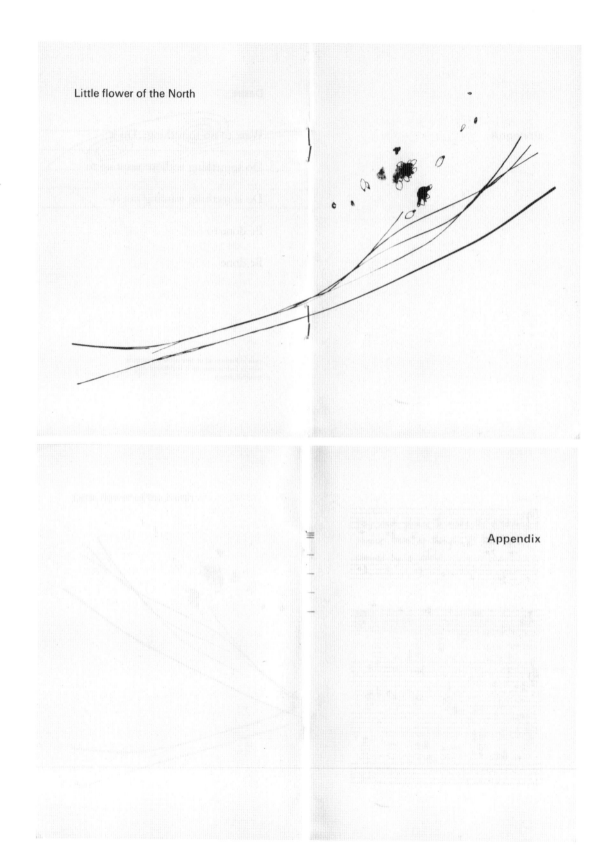

Appendix

play each phrase to make the preceding phrase seem as though it had been played by a child.

Triad

Guidelines for systematic interpretations of the triangles

As a △ approaches the equilateral its duration tends to infinity. Ie, the *regularity* of the △ determines its duration:

equilateral △ = infinite duration;
isoseles △ = medium duration;
scalene △ = short duration;
obtuse angle △ = very short duration.

    Size of △ may determine loudness: very small △ is very loud; large △ is soft.

    Modes of progression from one △ to another:

1) Pass through a corner, The two △s have a point in common, which may be evaluated as one item of invariance from one triad and the next.
2) Slide along one side. The two △s have a continuous line in common

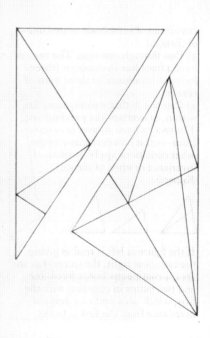

(two items of invariance or two units of silence.)

3) Pass through one side. The two △s have a fixed line in common (three items of invariance or three units of silence.)

4) Pass to a △ that encompasses, lies within, or overlaps the previous one. The two △s have an area in common (four — plus however many of the other conditions apply — items of invariance or units of silence).

Example:

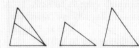

If the figure at left is read as giving the two △s at right, the second has an area, a continuous line, a fixed line and two points in common with the first, which adds up to 11 items of invariance from the first △ to the

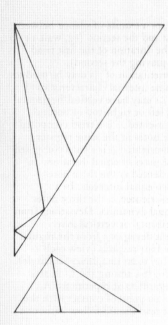

second, or 11 units of silence between the first and the second (eg, wait 11 times the duration of the first triad before playing the second).

Orientation of △s may be used to determine internal characteristics of triads. △s may have vertical/horizontal lines at left or right/top or bottom. A left-oriented △ is a triad composed of three notes in the same register. A right-oriented △ is a triad composed of three notes of equal duration. In a top-oriented △ the three notes form two equal intervals. In a bottom-oriented △ the three notes have equal dynamics. Deviations from the horizontal or vertical may represent deviations from the regular in these four respects (view each △ in relation to an imaginary rectangle).

Progress among the △s in any way, regardless of repetitions. A △ that has no point of contact with the one just read should follow without a

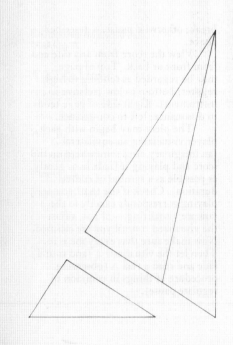

break; otherwise pause as described above.

View the score from any side and from front or back. Top of page may be regarded as tending to high register; bottom to low (relative to instrument). Right side of page tends to dissonance; left to consonance.

The piece may begin with each player visualizing an equilateral △ (an imaginary one) somewhere on the score and playing it (fade in as gently as possible as a symbol of endless duration). Check if the triad you are playing corresponds exactly to the △ you are visualizing — if not, adjust the visualized △ until you are satisfied. Now make sure that everyone is in. Then let the visualized △ (and sound) fade and read a real △ (observing procedure of things in common to regulate pause).

Properties required for Making A

A-gauge glass

White line

Glass bamer

Wet B

C-measure

Plenty of C

Plenty of dry A

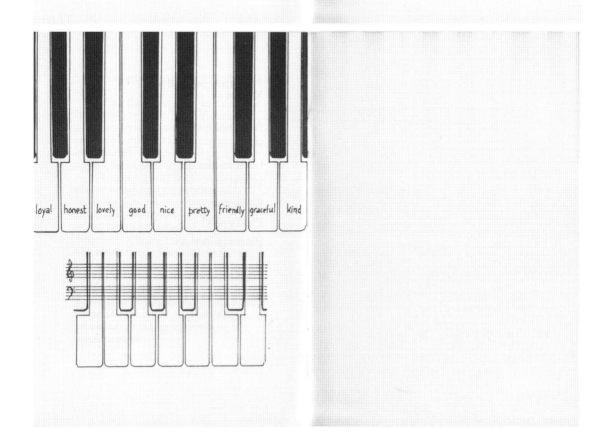

loyal | honest | lovely | good | nice | pretty | friendly | graceful | kind

The Scratch Orchestra and Visual Arts

Michael Parsons

In his essay 'Towards an Ethic of Improvisation', written shortly before the formation of the Scratch Orchestra, Cornelius Cardew said of performances of his graphic score *Treatise* (1963–7): 'Ideally such music should be played by a collection of musical innocents [people who had no formal musical training].' He continued, 'My most rewarding experiences with *Treatise* have come through people who by some fluke have (a) acquired a visual education, (b) escaped a musical education and (c) have nevertheless become musicians, i.e. play music to the full capacity of their beings.'[1]

The formation of the Scratch Orchestra in 1969 may be seen as the culmination of Cardew's search for new types of performer, from backgrounds other than that of a classical training. Performances of *Treatise* had taken place in art colleges during the 1960s, and more recent works such as his *Schooltime Compositions* (1967) also offered opportunities for visual as well as musical interpretation. Cardew's own involvement with the visual arts was close: during the 1960s he worked as a graphic designer, his wife Stella was a painter, and his circle of friends and colleagues included conceptual and performance artists such as George Brecht and Robin Page (both teaching at Leeds College of Art in the late 1960s), Mark Boyle, who was working with light projections, the painters Tom Phillips and Noel Forster and many others.

This was a period of far-reaching change and innovation in British art schools. The academic disciplines of life-drawing, figurative composition and illustration and the traditional craft-based skills, which had been central to art education since the mid-19th century, were being challenged by new attitudes and policies that reflected some of the more radical tendencies in 20th-century art. Leading artist educators such as Victor Pasmore and Harry Thubron introduced enquiry into fundamental aspects of perception and expression, structure and method, and students were encouraged to experiment freely with materials of all kinds. Boundaries between disciplines were questioned and redefined, and there was a shift from the object-based practices of painting and sculpture to an emphasis on process and context, environmental activity and time-based work in film, sound and performance. These changes began to take effect in the early 1960s following recommendations for the liberalisation of art education included in the Coldstream Report; a generation of artists emerged whose work extended into new material and conceptual areas.[2]

Visual Influences

The breaking down of barriers between different disciplines and the growth of interest among visual artists in sound and performance created a favourable climate for the development of experimental music. Cornelius Cardew, John Tilbury, David Bedford and other musicians were regular visitors at art colleges in and around London, in Leeds, Liverpool, Maidstone, Falmouth, Portsmouth and elsewhere. They not only performed and discussed the new music but also involved students as active participants in works by John Cage, Christian Wolff, Morton Feldman, Cardew, George Brecht, La Monte Young, Toshi Ichiyanagi, Takehisa Kosugi and other Fluxus-related composers. As a result, there soon arose an extended network of visually aware performers, for whom the lack of conventional musical training was no obstacle to participation in experimental music; many of these were among the original members of the Scratch Orchestra.[3]

Cardew's particular achievement at this time was to bring together visual artists and musicians from diverse backgrounds in situations to which all could contribute equally, regardless of skill or experience, with aural and visual aspects of performance coexisting in heterogeneous juxtaposition and interaction with each other. This diversity s reflected in the Draft Constitution, where Cardew notes: 'The word music and its derivatives are here not understood to refer exclusively to sound and related phenomena (hearing, etc.). What they do refer to is flexible and depends entirely on the members of the Scratch Orchestra.'[4]

John Cage and Fluxus

The immediate precedent for such an open-ended definition of music can, of course, be found in Cage's work of the 1950s and 1960s, in his collaborations with Merce Cunningham, Robert Rauschenberg and other artists, and in his idea of indeterminacy. His 'silent' piece *4'33"* (1952) had demonstrated that silence was not merely the absence of intentional sounds; it created a framework and focus of attention in which the listener is invited to redefine the significance of visual as well as aural aspects of musical performance. It thus opened the way to an area of intermediate activity through which there is no clear separation between seeing and hearing: both are essential aspects of any live performance situation. Cage's work of the 1950s and 1960s developed from the idea that different kinds of activity could coexist and interpenetrate without interference. A key occasion was that of the 'untitled event' that Cage organised in 1952 at Black Mountain College in North Carolina, which included live and recorded music, dance, poetry, painting, film and slide projections and a lecture by Cage himself. Each of these independent elements was assigned its own time-bracket within the total duration: Cage provided a rhythmic structure to indicate when and for how long each element was to take place, so that periods of activity and inactivity combined and overlapped in various ways. This event was followed by further works in which Cage reached far beyond conventional definitions of music to include disparate elements of all kinds: in his *Theatre Piece* (1960), for example, performers are asked to select their own repertories of materials and activities, which are individually programmed (in accordance with the directions of the numerical score) and presented simultaneously to create maximum visual and aural diversity.

Cage's experimental music course at the New School for Social Research in New York in 1958 attracted visual and performance artists and writers such as George Brecht, Allan Kaprow, Al Hansen, Dick Higgins and Jackson MacLow, many of whom became closely associated with Fluxus in the 1960s. Fluxus was an international movement with interconnected groups of participants in the USA, Germany, France, Japan and elsewhere, involving artists, writers, performers, musicians and others whose work could not easily be categorised within conventional boundaries. It was concerned with (among other things) a kind of art that would merge almost imperceptibly with everyday life: redefining perception of ordinary objects and events, reassessing the value of common materials, activities and situations. There was a prevailing interest in the use of chance, in games, puzzles and paradoxes, in inversions of conventional use and value that owed something to Dada and Surrealism, in particular to the work of Kurt Schwitters, Man Ray and Marcel Duchamp. A work of Ray's, *Object for Destruction* (1932) – also known as *Indestructible Object* – consists of the image of an eye, cut out from a photograph and attached with a paper clip to the arm of a metronome; this seems to prefigure Fluxus, with its play of meaning on references to seeing and hearing, its paradoxical title and its ambiguous status as either object or process (Ray explained that it was the idea that was indestructible, not the object itself, which could be remade any number of times). Another relevant work by Man Ray is his *Cadeau* (1921), a flat-iron with a row of tin tacks glued to its surface, perhaps inspired by Erik Satie. Just as the use of everyday objects and materials in the work of visual artists created shifts and transformations of meaning, so in the activities of Cage and Fluxus participants, traditional categories of music, sound and performance were subjected to radical disruption and redefinition.

The Japanese composers Toshi Kosugi and Takehisa Ichiyanagi brought a subtle and elusive quality to their pieces through the displacement of familiar activities. Kosugi's *Anima 7* (1964) states that a chosen action is to be performed 'as slowly as possible', and his *Theatre Music* (1964) instructs the performer to 'keep walking intently'. Ichiyanagi's *Distance* (1962) specifies that instruments are to be placed at least three metres away from the performers, who are required to play them from positions high up in the space: the effect is to inhibit the players' control over their instruments and to emphasise the disjunction between visual aspects of their actions and the fragmented sounds that result from this oblique approach to playing technique. The Scratch Orchestra performed this work at the International Students House in London on 9 April 1970, playing instruments by remote control from high platforms with ropes, rods, tubes, missiles and other specially devised equipment.

Brecht and Young

The work of George Brecht and La Monte Young, both closely associated with New York Fluxus in the early 1960s, was particularly influential in the development of the Scratch Orchestra. Brecht's *Water Yam* (1960–3) is a large collection of pieces published in New York by George Maciunas in the form of a box containing white cards, each of which carries a visual image or a few words that minimally specify or suggest an object, activity or event of some kind. Some of them refer to musical instruments – *Flute Solo*: 'disassembling/assembling'; *Solo for Violin* (or other string instrument): 'polishing'; *String Quartet*: 'shaking hands'. Others are concerned with the timing of chance occurrences (*Three Telephone Events*), or with non-musical sound sources (*Drip Event*, *Comb Music*). Brecht's pieces operate in an intermediate zone between object and event. Seeing and hearing are equally relevant to their interpretation: they may be realised as performances in any medium or they may be treated purely as observations or mental images. In the 1960s, Cardew and Tilbury often included in recitals Brecht's *Incidental Music* (1961), a work that deals with the piano as a physical object rather than as a sound source. Various activities are specified, to be performed in and around the piano; any sound that may arise from this activity is literally 'incidental'.[5]

In many respects, the all-inclusive spirit of Fluxus can be seen to anticipate that of the Scratch Orchestra: 'Artists, anti-artists, non-artists, anartists, the politically committed and the apolitical, poets of non-poetry, non-dancers dancing doers, undoers, non-doers: Fluxus encompasses opposites.'[6]

In a series of concerts organised by Cardew at the Commonwealth Institute, London, in April 1967, simultaneous performances were given of pieces by Cage, Brecht and Young: while Cage's *Variations I* was in progress, Robin Page interpreted Brecht's *Two Durations* (1960–1) ('red, green'), swinging coloured light bulbs on long flexes across the front of the stage, and John Tilbury performed Young's *Piano Piece for David Tudor No.1* (1960) ('Bring a bale of hay and a bucket of water onto the stage for the piano to eat and drink'), cooking a meal for himself while waiting for the piano's response ('The piece is over … after the piano eats or decides not to.') Young's *Poem for Tables*, *Chairs*, *Benches*, *Etc. (or other sound sources)* (1960) featured prominently among the works performed by the Scratch Orchestra in 1969 and 1970. In its original form, friction sounds were to be produced by pulling, pushing or dragging articles of furniture across the floor surface, according to a strictly programmed time-scheme determined by a selection of random numbers. In later versions, as described by Cardew, it developed into 'a kind of chamber opera, in which *any* activity, not necessarily even of a sounding variety, could constitute one strand in the complex weave of the composition'.[7] Another piece of Young's, open equally to visual or musical interpretation, was his *Composition 1960 No.10* ('Draw a straight line and follow it'), which could be performed as a single long-sustained tone or as any single-minded, undeviating linear activity. These and other Fluxus-related works were accessible to musically untrained performers, offering a different kind of challenge; they called for alternative skills of inventiveness, ingenuity, practicality and self-discipline, and total commitment to the task at hand in the face of any eventuality (including adverse audience reaction, interruption and even interference).

Multiplicity – Materiality

The coexistence of diverse strands of aural and visual activity was characteristic of many of the earlier concerts given by the Scratch Orchestra. The resulting multiplicity often has more in common with principles associated with visual arts, such as collage and assemblage, than with traditional musical methods; the complex intermixture of Scratch music, improvisation rites, compositions and fragments of popular classics emphasised the materiality of sound itself rather than the intentions of any single individual group within the orchestra. Whereas Cage, even in his most radical works of the 1950s and 1960s, still retained the role of the composer in controlling the formal outlines (if not the content) of simultaneous layers, the Scratch Orchestra's more collective approach to performance reflected its loose and informal sociability, which was based on mutual respect and tolerance rather than on adherence to any preconceived structure or set of rules.

The orchestra took part in a range of environmental events in London between 1969 and 1972, in streets, playgrounds, derelict sites and shopping centres, at Euston Railway Station, on the underground, on Hampstead Heath, Primrose Hill and the Regent's Park boating lake, and in Cornwall, North Wales, Northumbria and in isolated coastal areas and parts of the countryside. In August 1970, a simultaneous exchange took place with the New Zealand branch of the Scratch Orchestra, founded by Philip Dadson, who had been a participant in Cardew's experimental music class at Morley College (1968–9). The New Zealand group, based in the Fine Arts department at the University of Auckland, performed an annual open-air drumming event during the early 1970s in the volcanic crater of Mount Eden to mark the summer solstice, and in 1971 Dadson jointly coordinated a global event, *Earthworks*, with groups around the world simultaneously observing and recording local conditions to mark the September equinox at the moment of sunrise (NZ)/sunset (UK).[8] This interest in spatial and environmental context and in the characteristics of different locations reveals an affinity with the work of artists such as Walter de Maria, Robert Smithson and Lawrence Weiner in the USA and Richard Long, Hamish Fulton and Andy Goldsworthy in the UK, whose activities extended far beyond the confines of the gallery or museum. The speculative nature of the Research Project (as described in the Draft Constitution) and the idea of performances based on journeys (real or imaginary) also owe something to the conceptual art of the 1960s.[9]

The first Scratch performance to be based on the Research Project *Journey of the Isle of Wight Westwards by Iceberg to Tokyo Bay* was given at Chelsea Town Hall on 15 November 1969. Brecht was living in London at this time, and he participated in several Scratch Orchestra events during 1969 and 1970. On this occasion, the performance was inspired by a proposal from 'Brecht & MacDiarmid Research Associates' for the translocation of land masses by harnessing them to icebergs, the latest in an increasingly ambitious series of 'translocation and delivery' projects on which Brecht was working during the 1960s. It represents another aspect of his conceptual imagination, this time on a grand scale, in an area intermediate between practical engineering and pure speculation.

The feasibility of transporting icebergs from the polar regions to supply fresh water to desert areas of the world had apparently been discussed in scientific journals, and Brecht's proposal simply took the idea a stage further. In the year of the first American moon landing, it may not have seemed particularly far-fetched, perhaps suggesting an ironic comment on the lavish expenditure of resources for purely spectacular or symbolic effect. The Scratch Orchestra responded with a mixed-media extravaganza of typically divergent aural and visual activities, derived in various obscure ways from the research of individual participants. A collective 'splash and drip' painting on a long paper scroll evolved spontaneously in response to the instrumental sounds, in reversal of the usual relationship between music and visual stimulus of a graphic score such as *Treatise*. Brecht himself delivered a lecture on his investigations into certain relevant geographical, oceanographical, sociological, economic and political questions raised by the enterprise.

'Any Activity Whatsoever'

Painting as performance had its place as one activity among others, but it enjoyed no privileged status; interaction between sound and visual media took many different forms. In a performance of *Treatise* at Morley College in 1969, Tim Mitchell made a three-dimensional realisation of one page of the score in the form of a wooden relief structure: the sounds of nailing, sawing and drilling were his contribution to the music. A Fluxus-like interest in everyday activities, redefined and transposed into the context of performance, was much in evidence. A glance through *Scratch Music* and *Nature Study Notes* reveals many examples of such activities: standing, sitting, walking, running, jumping, smoking, washing, shaving, hair-cutting, eating, drinking, sweeping, ball-bouncing, stone-throwing, measuring, counting, inventing and playing games of various kinds – the list could be extended *ad infinitum*[10]. All these and more were liable to occur in performance. Michael Chant's *Pastoral Symphony*, an abstruse verbal score written in 1969 shortly before the formation of the orchestra, generalised this tendency to the extent of specifying as its material 'any activity whatsoever involving two or more persons.'[11]

The *1001 Activities* of the Slippery Merchants, a picaresque sub-group within the orchestra dedicated to evading or subverting all remaining vestiges of musical authority, consisted of a bizarre list of puns, parodies and gags, a comprehensive (and sometimes incomprehensible) *reductio ad absurdum* of performance instructions, e .g . '**41** Travel a short distance on knees … **44** Funny laugh plus silly walk … **71** Throw many things far and wide … **79** Insult someone … **206** Stamp foot … **585** Sing Balls to the Baker, arse against the wall.'[12] Some of these erupted during the Journey performance at the Queen Elizabeth Hall, London, on 2? November 1970 (*Pilgrimage from Scattered Points on th Surface of the Body to the Brain, the Inner Ear, the Hear and the Stomach*), in defiance of more or less conventionall disciplined forms of presentation.

Visual activities and games of various kinds were includec by Cardew in the Action Score of 'Paragraph 5' of *The Grea Learning* (1968–70) in an attempt to incorporate anc restrain some of the more anarchic tendencies: he describec 'Paragraph 5' as representing his own view of the diversity of the orchestra with its 'high level of differentiation o actions and functions'.[13] There is much material of primarily visual interest in 'Paragraph 5', including the Dumb Show, with its repertory of gestures adapted from American Indiar sign language, and *Silent Music* (one of seven verbal compositions included in *The Great Learning*, 'Paragraph 5'), with its instruction 'No sound. Silent and still. Occasionally a movement watched by all, never more than one at a time. Sit in a semicircle like sculptured Pharaohs … Very heavy music.'

Just as 'any activity whatsoever' could be included in the category of performance, so any kind of graphic material came to be regarded as a possible form of notation: a look at *Scratch Music* reveals a miscellany of drawings, diagrams, maps, collages, texts, photographs and found objects (even some musical notation) from the notebooks of 16 members of the orchestra, laid out in random juxtaposition to suggest the visual equivalent of a Scratch performance. Anything that could be set down on paper, it seemed, could become part of the all-inclusive and indiscriminate category of 'graphic music'. Any kind of text or image came to be regarded as a possible incentive to performance, with rules for interpretation either left completely open or implicitly suggested, as in Tom Phillips's *Postcard Compositions* (op. XI): 'Buy a postcard. Assume that it depicts the performance of a piece. Deduce the rules of the piece. Perform it.'[14]

Events and Situations

Phillips had become involved with experimental music during the 1960s through his association with Cardew and Tilbury; he made frequent allusion in his paintings and drawings to musical processes and materials and developed a variety of oblique approaches to representation through the use of found imagery, text, calligraphy and musical notation. He made graphic scores such as *Four Pieces for John Tilbury* (1966) and *Gapmap* (1968), a drawing consisting of a row of vertical lines at chance-determined intervals: this was done for Brian Eno, then a student at Winchester School of Art, to determine the time-structure of a performance.

Visual events linked different occasions and locations: Stefan Szczelkun's silver disc, first seen against the sky suspended in a rocky cleft in a quarry in Cornwall, reappeared later in a concert performance at Ealing Town Hall, London (1971). Among other pieces of primarily visual interest was Catherine Williams's *String Games* (1971), for groups of women weaving spatial patterns with continuous lengths of string, passing them from hand to hand and then reversing the process.[15] My own *Walk* (1969), for any number of people walking in a large public space, was performed in the forecourt at Euston Railway Station, London (23 May 1970), and elsewhere; this involved walkers individually criss-crossing the space at different randomly determined speeds waiting for different lengths of time at chosen points and then setting off in another direction.[16] At Euston, this naturally intersected with the activities of *bona fide* travellers as they hurried or waited for their trains.

In addition to more-or-less planned events, there was also a variety of informal activity, often spontaneous and unrecorded, which arose in response to circumstances, crossing formal boundaries and spilling over into everyday life, especially in street performances, as during the *Richmond Journey* in May 1970: walking backwards or crawling through a shopping centre, handing out leaves in a supermarket, improvising on underground trains, a tug-of-war, ball game or other impromptu activity.

Changing Direction

In the summer of 1971, internal dissension about the orchestra's role and policy began to emerge, and a 'discontent' file was opened, in which members were encouraged to express their disagreements and criticisms. Energies were refocused on building a 'Scratch cottage' as part of the International Art Spectrum exhibition at Alexandra Palace, North London, a temporary construction collectively assembled from found materials to a plan by Stefan Szczelkun. It housed the *Refuse Collection* of paintings, collage and assemblages by members of the orchestra and provided an informal space for performance and discussion over a two-week period in August 1971. The search for a new socially committed role gathered support; members worked collectively on the composition of a Scratch opera, *Sweet FA* (1971–2), depicting scenes from the orchestra's clash with police and officials at the Newcastle Civic Centre in July 1971. This marked the transition from a diverse range of anarchist and libertarian attitudes and sympathies to a more specifically political (Maoist) outlook; visual talents were redirected to functional, 'agitprop' uses – designing posters, banners and painted backdrops.

The Portsmouth Connection

Meanwhile, in the Department of Fine Art at Portsmouth Polytechnic, the new emphasis on diversity in art education gave rise to a unique set of conditions for the development of experimental music.[17] On the initiative of Jeffrey Steele, Maurice Dennis and visiting artists such as Noel Forster and David Saunders, a strong theoretical and administrative basis for the inclusion of music in the Fine Art course was established in 1968. First Ron Geesin, then Gavin Bryars, was appointed lecturer in music, and in 1970, when Bryars moved to Leicester, I took over his position on a part-time basis. There were regular visits to Portsmouth by Cardew and Tilbury, John White, Christopher Hobbs, Howard Skempton and other members of the Scratch Orchestra.

Opportunities for working together on musical projects, offering a marked contrast to individual studio-based painting and sculpture, were seized upon with enthusiasm by an unusually energetic and imaginative group of students.

The Portsmouth Sinfonia was formed in May 1970 with the avowed aim to perform popular classical pieces as accurately as possible with players of limited technical ability and experience. Some of them were complete beginners who acquired second-hand instruments specially to take part in the Sinfonia's performances, learning through trial and error as they went along; their commitment and enthusiasm more than made up for the lack of conventional skills. Technical shortcomings were here turned to positive advantage as an agent of transformation, and processes of deviation and decontrol – long regarded as legitimate in the visual arts (in the works of Jackson Pollock, Willem de Kooning, Jasper Johns and Robert Rauschenberg, for example) – were transposed into a musical context, with unexpected and often hilarious results.

While it shared much of the general background of the Scratch Orchestra, music at Portsmouth soon developed its own distinctive characteristics, arising from the convergence of several currents of thought and practice in music and visual arts. The presence of Gavin Bryars, recently returned from working in the USA with Cage, acted as catalyst: he introduced students to a wide range of new music, including that of Cage, Brecht, Young, Lucier, Ichiyanagi and various Fluxus composers. His own work at this time was largely conceptual and speculative, often deliberately proposing improbable situations and conditions of performance in which results were bound to exceed or fall short of intentions.[18] In his lecture course *System and the Artist* (1969–70), Jeffrey Steele discussed formal systems and rule-governed procedures, taking into account how deviations could arise from following through a rational programme of decision-making; the 'optical' effects that arose in his own paintings in the 1960s, for example, were regarded as interesting side effects rather than intentional results of the use of systems. Noel Forster gave a lecture, 'The Painting as a Measure of Its Own Performance' (1970) in which he described ways in which error and deviation from a planned programme contributed to the development of his own work. John Tilbury worked with students on pieces from Brecht's *Water Yam*, many of which dealt with visual aspects of musical performance; soon pianos, violins and other instruments, displaced from their customary functions, began to appear as visual objects in films made at Portsmouth. The students became familiar, through Bryars, with Cage's reappropriation of classical material in works such as *HPSCHD* (1967) and with the work of John White, Christopher Hobbs and other English composers who were using found musical material from various sources. Further encouragement, if any were needed, was provided by the section on popular classics in Cardew's Draft Constitution. Exception was taken, however, to the phrase 'filling in gaps with improvised variational material': in performances by the Portsmouth Sinfonia, there was no improvisation as such, but always an attempt to play as accurately as possible, given the circumstances; variation arose naturally from differences of ability and from the wide disparity between intentions and results.

The Portsmouth Sinfonia soon outgrew its art-school origins and expanded to include a wide range of artists and musicians including (among others) Brian Eno, Steve Beresford, Michael Nyman and Barry Flanagan. It achieved extensive publicity and a degree of notoriety in a series of concerts in London and elsewhere, culminating in a performance at the Royal Albert Hall on 28 May 1974. Its success owed as much to visual as to musical characteristics: to its colourful and heterogeneous stage presence and air of professional confidence, to the incongruity of the expectations it aroused and to the flamboyance of its conductor John Farley, whose visual flair far outweighed his lack of technical competence and his inability to read a score. Such an enterprise is unthinkable outside the broad context of visual and performance art, in which there is a long history of interest in mistakes, accidents and deviations from recognised structure reaching back to the early years of Dada and Surrealism, to the work of Jean Arp, Kurt Schwitters, Francis Picabia and Marcel Duchamp, for which there is no exact precedent or parallel in the history of music.

While it was certainly the most widely publicised, the Sinfonia was by no means the only group to emerge from the Department of Fine Art in Portsmouth at this time. For example, there was the Ross and Cromarty Orchestra, formed in 1970 by Ivan Hume Carter to perform pieces of exemplary simplicity for players of elementary technical skill.

Conflicting Impulses

The Ross and Cromarty Orchestra was disbanded in 1972 as a result of political tensions and disagreements similar to those that affected the Scratch Orchestra. Hume Carter repudiated his previous involvement with the Sinfonia and other experimental activities and, like Cardew and others, turned to writing music intended to serve proletarian interests. Another group made up largely of Portsmouth musicians was the Majorca Orchestra, a chamber ensemble formed in 1972. Their undeviating renderings of straightforward melodies, and refusal in this context of any suggestion of irony or caricature, were in marked contrast to the performances of the Sinfonia, of which they were also members; here their approach emulated the new-found interest in melodic immediacy of pieces such as Skempton's *Waltz* (1970), or John Tilbury's rediscovery of the popular appeal of Albert W. Ketèlbey's *Bells across the Meadows* (1921).[19]

Discipline and Freedom

Within the Scratch Orchestra also, in contrast to the loosely structured character of many of the earlier events, there was an opposing tendency towards more disciplined forms of music-making. For many of the composers involved, these tendencies were complementary rather than in conflict with each other; the apparent contradiction between control and freedom gave rise to challenges that were positively stimulating. Cardew had in 1968 organised the first British performances of Terry Riley's *In* C (1964) and La Monte Young's *Death Chant* (1961), works in which the use of elemental and static musical material and multiple repetition played a dominant role, and these features, alongside graphic and indeterminate notation, were also prominent in parts of *The Great Learning* and in compositions by other members of the orchestra. It was perhaps inevitable that the tendency towards anarchy in some of the early Scratch performances should provoke a counter-reaction, and a more controlled and determinate strand of compositional activity soon reasserted itself in the work of John White, Christopher Hobbs, Alec Hill, Hugh Shrapnel and Brian Dennis, amongst others, and also in my collaborations with Howard Skempton. White's 'machine' compositions were particularly influential in providing a counterbalance to the increasingly free and improvisatory tendencies in Cardew's own work. The early music of Steve Reich and Philip Glass was becoming known in Britain at this time, and there was a general sense of a return to fundamental musical procedures. The use of repetitive sequences and rhythmic systems is characteristic of much of the music of this period, and it was in this context that a different kind of relationship between composers and visual artists began to emerge.

Systems Art and Music

In 1971 an association was formed with artists of the Systems group, initially as a result of the Portsmouth connection, with Jeffrey Steele and David Saunders, and then with Malcolm Hughes, Jean Spencer, Peter Lowe, Michael Kidner and others. A concert was given in June 1971 at the Arnolfini Gallery in Bristol, in which Christopher Hobbs, Michael Nyman, Howard Skempton and I participated, with the matrix exhibition of visual works by Systems artists, and in 1972 the Promenade Theatre Orchestra (PTO) – a group of four composer-performers (Alec Hill, Christopher Hobbs,

Hugh Shrapnel and John White) playing their own composition on reed organs, toy pianos and percussion – performed in association with the *Systems* exhibition at the Whitechapel Art Gallery in London. At the same time, Brian Dennis was writing pieces influenced by the visual symmetry and repetitive patterns of painters such as Robin Denny and Bridget Riley. The use of geometrical forms, modular structures and the incremental progression of linear and spatial elements suggested a close parallel with similar musical processes.[20]

The terms of the relationship between the composers and artists of the Systems group were quite different from, indeed dramatically opposed to, those of concurrent Fluxus-related tendencies. Instead of involving the use of mixed media and the fusion of visual and musical elements, it was based on a common interest in structural principles. With a few notable exceptions, the artists were not directly involved as performers: collaboration took the form rather of exchanging and comparing ideas in discussions and informal meetings. The search for coherent connections took precedence over the acceptance of chance coincidences and arbitrary juxtapositions, and concerts and exhibitions were organised with related but separate presentations on visual and musical work. The primary concern was now with formal clarity, and from this point of view it was considered that, given the difference of medium between visual and musical works, the indiscriminate mixing of incompatible elements could only give rise to confusion. It was more satisfactory to try to respect the boundaries of each medium so that correspondences and parallels on the theoretical and structural level could become evident.

While this association with visual artists working in the tradition of European Constructivism arose partly as a reaction to contradictions within the Scratch Orchestra, it soon gained its own momentum and continued to develop independently throughout the 1970s and 1980s. For composers, it involved the process of redefining the limits of composition and establishing new structural disciplines. At a time when ideological divisions within the Scratch Orchestra were proving irreconcilable, it helped to provide an implicit critique of some of its more anarchic tendencies, from a formal and aesthetic rather than from a political point of view.

Conclusion

It is clear in retrospect that experimental music in Britain, as in the United States, has owed much of its distinctive character to the influence and example of developments in the visual arts. The principles of indeterminacy and open form, the use of collage and assemblage, of juxtaposition and simultaneity, the questioning of traditional hierarchies and values, the awareness of space and silence and the emphasis on texture and materiality of sound all reflect a close involvement with visual and spatial concepts. They offer radical alternatives to the conservatism of most other forms of contemporary music, which are still largely tied to narrative models of expressive rhetoric and linear continuity. It was this influx of ideas from outside the musical mainstream that enabled the Scratch Orchestra to break away from traditional notions of order and expression, and to realise briefly its utopian vision of open enquiry and unfettered exploration, of an all-inclusive form of social music-making and performance, illuminated by the spirit of irreverent humour, discovery and invention.

'The Scratch Orchestra and Visual Arts' has been edited for this publication. It first appeared in Leonardo Music Journal, Vol.11, pp.5–11, 2001.

Cornelius Cardew, 'Towards an Ethic of Improvisation' (1968) anthologised in his *Treatise Handbook* (London: Peters Edition, 1971).

First Report of the National Advisory Council on Art Education (London: Her Majesty's Stationary Office, 1960).

The Scratch Orchestra grew out of Cardew's experimental music class at Morley College (an adult education institute in South London). In addition to musical colleagues and students of Cardew (among them, Michael Chant, Christopher Hobbs, Richard Reason, Hugh Shrapnel, Howard Skempton, John Tilbury and John White) and improvisers (such as Lou Gare, Eddie Prévost and Keith Rowe), the original membership included many participants from the visual arts (Greg Bright, Psi Ellison, Judith Euren, Carole Finer, David and Diane Jackman, Tim Mitchell, Tom Phillips and Stefan Szczelkun). Among those who joined later were visual and performance artists such as Birgit Burckhardt and Catherine Williams. For its first two years, the orchestra flourished as an anarchic and loosely structured collective. In 1971 an ideological group was formed to study Marxist ideas and, after a struggle between opposing 'experimental' and 'political' factions, the orchestra abandoned experimentalism and devoted itself to specific political aims, in support of the British working class movement and the cause of Irish independence. It finally disbanded in 1974.

Cornelius Cardew, 'A Scratch Orchestra: Draft Constitution', *The Musical Times* (June 1969); reprinted in Cornelius Cardew (ed.), *Scratch Music* (London: Latimer New Directions, 1972).

For further information on the work of George Brecht, see Michael Nyman, *Experimental Music: Cage and Beyond* (London: Studio Vista, 1974); Michael Nyman, 'Interview with George Brecht', *Studio International*, November/December 1976 (*Art and Experimental Music* issue).

Unsigned Fluxus manifesto (probably by George Maciunas), *V TRE3* (New York: 1964).

Cornelius Cardew, 'The Sounds of La Monte Young', *London Magazine*, April 1967.

Philip Dadson, 'Earthworks' (1971), in Jim Allen and Wystan Curnow (eds.), *Some Recent New Zealand Sculpture and Post-Object Art* (Auckland: Heinemann, 1976).

Members of the orchestra were encouraged to keep a record of research into any subjects of their choice; results of this research were to be given 'musical realisation' (never clearly defined) – in so far as they seemed relevant to themes of performances based on the idea of a journey (as in the following example).

) Cornelius Cardew, *Scratch Music*; and Cornelius Cardew (ed.), *Nature Study Notes* (London: The Scratch Orchestra, 1969), containing the Scratch Orchestra's collection of 'improvisation rites'.

11 Michael Chant, *Pastoral Symphony* (1969), verbal score, in *Scratch Music*; reprinted in Nyman, *Experimental Music*.

12 The complete list of *1001 Activities* appears in *Scratch Music*.

13 This score was published in *Source, Music of the Avant Garde*, Issue 10 (1972).

14 Tom Phillips, *Postcard Compositions*, in *Scratch Music*.

15 Catherine Williams, 'String Games', in Cornelius Cardew (ed.), *Scratch Anthology of Compositions* (London: Scratch Orchestra, 1971).

16 Michael Parsons, 'Walk', in Nyman, *Experimental Music*.

17 See Jeffrey Steele, 'Collaborative Work at Portsmouth, *Studio International* (November/ December 1976).

18 Gavin Bryars (ed.), *Visual Anthology* (London: Experimental Music Catalogue, 1974).

19 John Tilbury included music by Ketèlbey in a recital at the Purcell Room (9 October 1970) as part of his series *Vola Solo*. Christopher Hobbs, in his programme note to this recital, discussed the rediscovery by English experimental musicians of popular music by earlier composers, 'satisfying as it does the desire for melody, harmony, nostalgia, all the qualities missing from Boulez, let us say)'.

20 See Michael Parsons, 'Systems in Art and Music', *The Musical Times* (October 1976).

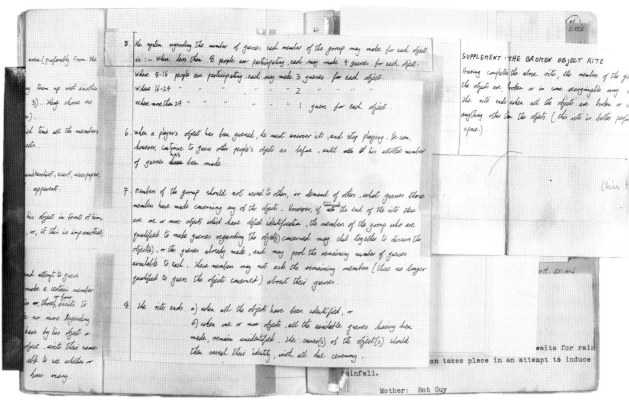

5. The system regarding the number of guesses each member of the group may make for each object is :- where less than 8 people are participating, each may make 4 guesses for each object.

Where 8-16 people are participating, each may make 3 guesses for each object.

Where 16-24 " " " " " " 2 "

Where more than 24 " " " " " " 1 guess for each object.

6. When a player's object has been guessed, he must uncover it, and stop playing. He can, however, continue to guess other people's objects as before, until all of his allotted number of guesses has been made.

7. Members of the group should not reveal to others, or demand of others, what guesses those members have made concerning any of the objects. However, if towards the end of the rite there are one or more objects which have defied identification, the members of the group who are qualified to make guesses regarding the object(s) concerned may club together to discuss the object(s), or the guesses already made, and may pool the remaining number of guesses available to each. These members may not ask the remaining members (those no longer qualified to guess the objects concerned) about their guesses.

8. The rite ends a) when all the objects have been identified, or
b) when one or more objects, all the available guesses having been made, remain unidentified. The owner(s) of the object(s) should then reveal their identity, with all due ceremony.

SUPPLEMENT: THE BROKEN OBJECT RITE

Having completed the above rite, the members of the gr... the objects are broken or in some recognizable way... The rite ends when all the objects are broken or... anything other than the objects (this rite is better perf... space).

waits for rain

...on takes place in an attempt to induce

rainfall.

Mother: Bob Guy

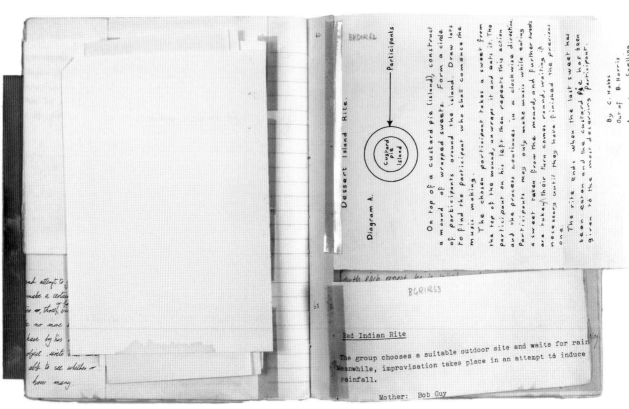

Dessert Island Rite

Diagram A.

Participants → Custard pie island

On top of a custard pie (island) construct a mound of wrapped sweets. Form a circle of participants around the island. Draw lots to find the participant who shall commence the music making.

The chosen participant takes a sweet from the top of the mound, unwraps it and eats it. The participant on his left then repeats this action and the process continues in a clockwise direction. Participants may only make music while eating a sweet taken from the mound, and further sweets are taken (their turn comes round) waiting, if necessary until they have finished the previous one.

The rite ends when the last sweet has been eaten and the custard pie has been given to the most deserving participant.

By C. Hobbs
Out of B. Harris

BWDIR 62

BGRIR 63

Red Indian Rite

The group chooses a suitable outdoor site and waits for rain
Meanwhile, improvisation takes place in an attempt to induce
rainfall.

Mother: Bob Guy

A small number of people arrange themselves in a circle. One person, using his voice only, makes a clear, easily imitable musical statement. He continues to repeat this statement for the duration of the whole 'first cycle' pausing freely between repeats. Meanwhile, the person immediately to the right of the first person listens carefully to the former's statement and memorises it. When he feels that he can reproduce it exactly with his own voice he does so adding to it his own simple musical statement. He continues to repeat this combined statement. Similarly the person just to the right of the second person listens, memorizes and executes vocally the whole combined statement of the second person to which he adds his own. Pauses, repeats, etc. The process continues until the evolving 'melody' is completed by the last person, once the repetitions of its parts.

At this point the second cycle begins. The last person repeats the whole melody as many times as there are participants. With each repeat he is joined in turn by the first, second, third etc. singing in unison with him and each other. During this cycle each person continues to 'sing' as described above until his turn to join the unison singing. The participants should seek to conserve their energies so that the unison singing is exuberant and joyous. People outside the circle may join in.

ACSRS14   "Sitting Room Song"   alyin curran 1969

CCAR17

Accompanying rite

At a signal all players commence playing a continuous accompaniment.

[An accompaniment is music that allows a solo — in the event of one being played — to be appreciated as such. Def.]

As the spirit moves them, individual players rise & play solos.

After soloing, rest.

After resting, play more accompaniment (the same or different).

Cease playing at a signal.

CC.
Srdla France.

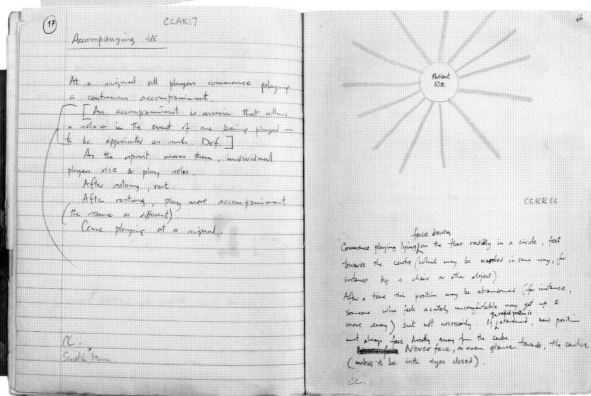

Radiant Rite

CCRR66

face down
Commence playing lying on the floor radially in a circle, feet towards the centre (which may be marked in some way, for instance by a chair or other object)

After a time this position may be abandoned (for instance, someone who feels acutely uncomfortable may get up & move away) but not necessarily. If abandoned, new position must always face directly away from the centre. Never face, or even glance towards, the centre (unless it be with eyes closed).

CC.

Nature Study Notes
Improvisation Rites 1969

No rights are reserved in this book of rites. They may be reproduced and performed freely. Anyone wishing to send contributions for a second set should address them to the editor: C. Cardew, 112 Elm Grove Road, London SW13.

For reasons of economy the pages of this book are re-produced from handwritten originals. The editor wishes to apologise for any inconvenience in reading caused by this method of production.

Nature Study Notes is referred to in the 'Draft Constitution of a Scratch Orchestra' (Musical Times, June 1969) and is currently in use by the Scratch Orchestra. Anyone wishing to take part in these rites or any other activities in the context of the Scratch Orchestra should write to the editor.

Nature Study Notes is published by the Scratch Orchestra and distributed by Experimental Music Catalogue, 26 Avondale Park Gardens, London W11.

Rites are printed in the approximate order of collection. Notes on the rites are in alphabetical order of code names. Many rites are accompanied by a pedigree naming one or more of the following: the Mother (her initials are at the head of the code name), who wrote it down as a rite; the Father (F:), who provided the idea; any other relatives the Mother sees fit to recall; and an Ancestor (A:) or Archetype, identifying the basic human or non-human state, activity or event that the rite bears on. In the notes there is no differentiation between the Mother's re-marks and those of the editor and others.

2

HSBR34 Six deep breaths......

BHWSR35 Think of a score and play it. If you can't think of one augment someone else's playing.

BHUSR36 Imagine a score and play it. If you can't imagine one, remain silent.

UNWWR37 Choose one of the following categories:
1) Christian names (male), 2) Christian names (female), 3) family names, 4) colors, 5) plants, 6) composers, 7) other.

Stand in a wide loose circle, as far away from one another as you can get without actually having to shout to make yourself heard. Beginning at any point in the circle, take turns naming, without hesitation, whatever word from the chosen category comes to mind. Speak loudly and clearly. If you feel like repeating a previous word, do so. The important thing is to keep the words coming until the winning word is spoken. Winning words are:
1) Wendell, 2) Martha, 3) Schwartz, 4) Green, 5) Carrots, 6) Offenbach, 7) freely chosen.
The first to speak the winning word (naturally) wins. As soon as you have won, go anywhere you like, and begin to play. If your victory was genuine, you may play as loudly as you wish. If your victory was fraudulent, you must play quietly throughout.

Meanwhile the person who was next you in the circle begins the game again, and so it goes until all are playing but one. This person, being the only non-winner, is the loser. Two courses of action are open to him: a) He may consider himself a fraudulent winner and play quietly, in which case the piece goes on for a predetermined length of time, and then stops. b) He may remain a loser, in which case everyone he touches must stop playing and become a loser likewise, with similar powers of conferring musical death by touch. When nothing but losers are left, the piece ends.

TMTTR38 Mark out a journey (inwardly/outwardly/

spatially). Make it.

TMCR39 A pack of cards is shuffled and laid face down. Each performer takes at least one card. When every performer has a card, improvisation can commence. Cards can be exchanged or discarded any number of times. Discarded cards are placed face up by the deck. When all the cards are discarded, activity ends.

TM40 Take a space. Make a sound in it. Make another sound in it. Make another sound in it. Get to know the space. Take an object. Do something to it. Do something else to it. Do something else to it. Do something else to it. Get to know the object. Take a person. Watch them make an action. Watch them make another action. Watch them make another action. Watch them make another action. Get to know the person. Do something. Do something else. Do something else. Do something else. Get to know yourself.

HSTPR41 Each player divides himself into three equal parts.

CCIR42 Perform a service for an individual or the group: pat them on the head, dress them, entertain them, educate

them, something. On recognizing a service performed for you, pay for it in music. You may pay for it immediately (in musical hard cash), or delay payment, in which case you have to pay interest. The interest increases in proportion to the length of the delay. Interest can accrue to the music in any dimension. In proportion as the interest approaches infinity, the situation approaches stability.

HMSIR43 Walk down the riverside path from Greenwich Pier, past the Naval College, the little Trinity Hospital, the Power Station, to the Gasworks at Woolwich, picking up en route odd items, such as driftwood, scrap metal, etc. Make sounds in any way with the items picked up.

HMSIR44 Do something impossible. Do something possible; Make the impossible thing seem possible, Make the possible thing seem impossible.

HMSBR45 Arrange to listen to a piece by Beethoven; exaggerate in some way (perhaps actively) what would be your normal emotional response to it. The piece itself may or may not form part of the improvisation.

MPPAYPR46 One person acts as money collector. To play, payment must be made at the following rates: 2 mins. – 6d. 5 mins. – 1/-. 10 mins – 2/-. 30 mins – 5/- 1 hour – 10/-. etc. The money collector must keep an eye on players to make sure they do not exceed their time, and to call them in when it is up. All payment must be made in advance. Money collected to go to the Scratch Orchestra A/c.

FRLMDP47 For any number of musicians playing melody instruments plus any number of non-musicians playing anything.

in each octave. Read from left to right, playing the notes as follows: 1, 1-2, 1-2-3, 1-2-3-4, etc. When you have reached note 65, play the whole melody once again and then begin subtracting notes from the beginning: 2-3-4...65, 3-4-5... 65, 4-5-6... 65, ..., 62-63-64-65, 63-64-65, 64-65, (65). Hold the last note until everybody has reached it, then begin an improvisation using any instruments. In the melody above, never stop or falter, always play loud. Stay together as long as you can, but if you get lost, stay lost. Do not try to find your way back into the fold. Continue to follow the rules strictly.

NON-MUSICIANS are invited to make sound, any sound, preferably very loud, and if possible are provided with percussive or other instruments. The non-musicians have a leader, whom they may follow or not, and who begins the music thus: (♩ = 150) ♫ ♫ ♫ ♫ .... etc. (f sempre). As soon as this pulse has been established any variations are possible.

HMSVR48 Members of the group each to perform some action while intermittently consuming a large bottle of Vodka. Actions made should preferably necessitate communication with other members of the group. Performance ends for each player when he has consumed the Vodka &/or is completely incapacitated.

The Time is Now, the Place is Everywhere

John Tilbury

My brief this morning, *Treatise*, Cardew's mammoth graphic score, seems to be quite circumscribed. However, because there *is* a seamless connection between all Cardew's activities, through a liberating, humanising quest to extend people's freedoms and sense of responsibilities, it is, I think, inevitable that we should stray into other areas outside and beyond the period when he was writing *Treatise* (1963–67).

Viewed chronologically, this quest began in the early 1960s, when Cardew devised new notations, liberating the performer from the constraints of serialism, which for him meant restoring the fragile and sometimes unreliable performer back to the hub of music-making – the performer as free, active, spontaneous human agency: works such as *Autumn '60* and *Octet for J.J.* Secondly, through the improvising group AMM, the quest to liberate the performer – that is, the conservatory-trained musician – from the constraints of the written score. Thirdly, with the Scratch Orchestra, to free people from the shackles of their musical education, when they had been deemed to be non-musical and virtually excluded from music-making. And fourthly, his espousal of Marxism-Leninism, through which the oppressed of the world would finally grasp their destiny with their own hands. Clearly, in any discussion about Cardew, there are no comfort zones. So let us begin with one of Cornelius's most compelling musical quotes:

> Notation is a way of making people move.[1]

'Making' was perhaps an inappropriate choice of word; it was not in Cardew's musical philosophy to *make* people *do* anything. And yet in the 1950s, the heyday of total serialism (with its scientific pretensions), with Boulez and Stockhausen at the helm, the relationship between composer and performer had indeed become a coercive one: play that loud, play that louder, do this softly, wait, stop. Notations had

become a sequence of commands. Nor, incidentally, did Cage resolve that contradiction.

The best contemporary composers, among whom I would include Christian Wolff and Cardew, notate *creatively*; they understand the idiosyncrasies, the contradictions, the limitations and inadequacies of notation. Notation's brief is human communication, which is fraught with difficulties and plagued by misunderstandings. Notation embodies a relationship between human beings; as a performer, somebody is inviting, cajoling, ordering, bribing me to carry out certain actions. In our society, the cash nexus is the dominant driving force, and therefore most of the music we hear is in the form of notated compositions performed by professionals or would-be professionals. (I remember Cornelius once saying, à propos of *Autumn '60*, 'Nobody can be involved with this music in a merely professional capacity.')

Treatise was the culmination of a trilogy of works (with *Autumn '60* and *Octet '61*) in which this essential, human dialogue was reopened, explored and refined. Rather than prescribing sounds, with *Treatise* Cardew sought to stimulate, provoke and inspire through a visual score of astonishing scope and imagination which, sometimes subtly, sometimes flagrantly, impinges on the performer's sensibilities, serving not simply as a measure of the performer's intellectual capacity, digital dexterity and viability, but also of her probity, of her virtuosity, courage, tenacity, alertness and so on (on which he was to call again a few years later with his *Schooltime Compositions*). And for Cardew, drawing *Treatise* was an integral part of the compositional process; he was aware of the psychological drama generated through the performer's relation to the (drawn) notation in the act of interpretation.

With *Treatise*, Cardew had set himself the task of deconstructing (not rejecting) musical notation (there *is* historical and stylistic sedimentation scattered throughout the score) in an attempt to lay bare the essential nature of the human relations embedded within it. Conventionally, the musical score represents a property relation – the composer wns the score; but it also embodies another more important relation, a relation *between* people, that of the composer to the performers. Moreover, through bar-line and baton, through the *notation*, the composer also governs the relationships between performers.

For a start, and quite radically, *Treatise* appeared in accordance with Cardew's wishes without any introductory material 'to mislead prospective performers into the slavish practice of doing what they are told'. Several years later, in 1971, the publication by Peters Edition of the *Treatise Handbook* did not really compromise his earlier position in relation to performer instruction, although the Journal of Working Notes, with which it begins, and the numerous aphorisms which spice it, provide a fascinating insight into Cardew's developing ideas on musical notation.

For Cardew, insight into the way of life of musicians was crucial to any understanding of the art they practise. He was deeply interested in the 'stream of life' within which musical utterances found expression (I recall his wonderful description of the music of La Monte Young performed in a London working-class pub), just as his silent mentor, Wittgenstein, would try to draw us away from words and sentences to consider rather the occasions on which we use them, the context which gives them a particular meaning.

Despite his frequent references in the earlier pages of the *Handbook* to the supremacy of the notation, Cardew now seemed to be suggesting, towards the end of 1966 and before the work was completed, that in the act of making music the score has no more 'authority' than any other parameter. For in *Treatise*, the notation does not depict, or attempt to depict, an existing sound 'reality'; it is there to inspire, even incite the performer in order to bring about a music which does not yet exist. In fact, this was a view he had reflected upon even in the early months: on 28 September 1963, in the *Treatise Handbook*, he remarked that in *Treatise* 'the score seems not representational. No rules of representation. Except the central line represents perhaps the performer or a single line

of thought'.[2] Notation could not be simply a representation of sounds any more than linguistic forms comprise solely statements of facts.

And yet, in *Treatise*, by prescribing no rules at all, Cardew brings the question of 'rules' to the surface; the performer is invited, by implication, or by default, to provide his own. Of course, different modes of procedure presuppose different perceptions, but even in the most spontaneous and wayward of interpretations (for example, where the performer responds to perceived changes in audience behaviour), rules and attitudes towards rules are invariably involved. It is the absence of *prescribed* rules which makes *Treatise* such a radical departure.

Through his creation of a notation which was about 'making people move', Cardew had to address the fundamental issues of why and how people *humanise* sounds, just as Wittgenstein had brought all the great philosophical questions which have arisen out of the various discourses to the same level from which philosophy started – ordinary human life. One may even conceptualise a musical language which has no rules at all, an internalised language embedded in life, in human activity – as in Cardew's later work *Schooltime Compositions*.

Cardew clearly relished these problems, not least because logic seemed to be under threat from art. In the following quote from the *Tempo* article, from the early 1960s, he seems to be expressing the same anthropological attitude to logic which had impressed him in Wittgenstein's *Philosophical Investigations*: 'Compare "that seems natural" with "that seems logical" with "there is a sort of severe logic in it" meaning it's not natural but it's "right".'[3] In the context of human affairs, logic appears less intractable, even vulnerable. For Cardew, the source of all rules and rule-making, of all necessities, is *in ourselves*; rules and their application are derived from our practice, our *modus vivendi*. For Cardew, in music they are derived from the requirements, the needs, of our music-making, not according to some external, musicological canon.

Treatise embodies a different set of relations: most importantly, it is a negation of the egocentricity that lies at the heart of Western artistic orthodoxy. Because *Treatise* does not wholly belong, either to Cardew or to those whose lives it nourishes and inspires, it is offered and shared unconditionally, untethered to any rules or laws of musical composition or any other 'figments of the musicological imagination'.[4] What Cardew proposes to the performer in *Treatise* is no less than a voyage of 'self-invention' (to borrow from Eddie Prévost): 'What I hope is that in playing this piece (*Treatise*) each musician will give of his own music – he will give it as his response to my music, which is the score itself.'[5] And it was the ethos of 'self-invention' which became the categorical imperative of Cardew's revolutionary musical thought and practice in those heady years of the late 1960s – with AMM and with the Scratch Orchestra. So by the time *Treatise* was nearing completion, Cardew's attitude towards it was decidedly anthropocentric:

> Each player interprets the score according to his own acumen and sensibility. He may be guided by many things – by the internal structure of the score itself, by his personal experience of music-making, by reference to the various traditions growing up around this and other indeterminate works, by the action of the other musicians working on the piece, and – failing these – by conversation with the composer during rehearsal.[6]

And by this time, in 1966, and this is perhaps the crux of the matter, Cardew was already a fully fledged member of AMM; moreover, he expressed the view that an improvisatory character was essential to *Treatise*. This was a clear shift in his thinking for which a newly discovered, serious commitment to free improvisation was a key contributory factor. Initially, he had insisted that the score must govern the music; it was not an arbitrary jumping-off point for improvisation, although this, in fact, is what it became for many interpreters; the majority found it simply more practical, and less daunting, to adopt an impressionistic attitude towards *Treatise*. And yet, as late as 1970, Cardew still seemed unsure as to the precise nature of this 'improvisatory quality'. On the one hand, he did not consider *Treatise* 'improvisatory', and yet, I quote,

> It does seem (using hindsight) to have pointed in the direction of improvisation. A square musician (like myself) might use *Treatise* as a path to the ocean of spontaneity.[7]

It is a profound irony that Cardew's involvement with AMM and improvised music began at a time when his mastery of the misconceived, misused art of musical notation had, with *Treatise*, reached a peak. For while he was seeking to refine the art of notation, his actual music-making, with AMM, drew him ineluctably to its abandonment. For a time they coexisted, uneasily; for performances of *Treatise* could not measure up to the extraordinary soundscapes of AMM's world. Musically, *Treatise* lived in the shadow of AMM, and it was the fabulous visual presence of the score which alone guaranteed its unassailable position in contemporary music. An imaginative, silent, lone reading of *Treatise* was an experience which even an AMM performance could not surpass; it was through *Treatise* that Cardew clung on to notation. He was still convinced of the broader significance of notation as a paradigm of communication between people rather than as a crude and unwieldy symbolisation of sounds.

Of course, the notion of 'communication between people' itself begs unsettling questions, for if Cardew devised a system through which notational control mechanisms could be loosened, it was never his intention that they should be relinquished altogether. 'Control is essential to authority', Eddie Prévost has reminded us, and the bug of 'authority' had bitten deep into Cardew, however generously one chooses to interpret manifestations of it at crucial stages of his career: the Scratch Orchestra, *The Great Learning*, and Leninism.[8] At the same time it is emblematic of this complex and unfathomable man that he should have placed a Taoist text at the heart of the Confucian Great Learning in 'Paragraph 5' of *The Great Learning*.

and what about playing, performing *Treatise*? What is it like? What does it involve?

To read and act upon a notation can be a liberating experience; a notation can posit the unthinkable, the unimaginable, the unplayable, the unperformable, just as Cage's and Wolff's notations sometimes do. In *Treatise*, too, the signs expand the normal field of reference of traditional notation beyond the received definitions of 'music'. *Treatise* cannot be circumscribed by purely musical references; *Treatise* invites us, irresistibly, to play, to sing – but also to dance (dancers have been inspired to choreograph their readings of *Treatise*), to perform, to act, to move; ultimately, to *self-invent*. With *Treatise*, Cardew wanted to incite the performer to risk, to transgress, not through an 'accident' thrown up by the score, as in Cage, but through the redefinition, the reinvention, of her own consciousness.

For musicians involved in both reading and improvising, it is instructive to contrast playing *Treatise* with improvising; in improvisation, the stimulus to play and to continue playing is generated from within, in response to the music as it unfolds, and the music develops organically; in *Treatise*, the listener is intensely aware of a *third force*, an authority which impinges upon the music-making, obliging the performer to stop playing where she might prefer to continue, or to go off on a new tack where she might prefer to remain where she is, or suddenly to introduce a contrasting instrumental technique at a juncture where it feels inappropriate. Thus for the listener there can be a disorientating feeling of arbitrariness, of insecurity or, more positively, of unexpectedness; the influence of the score appears now benign, now malevolent. Eddie Prévost illustrates this 'third force' in more personal terms; for that reason, perhaps, his words produce a stronger, more lasting resonance. Whereas the investigative mode and dialogue are the dominant features of improvised music (at least, we should add, in Prévost's preferred practice), with *Treatise*, I quote:

Tracking the score, allowing its presence, history and associations to permeate the music, inevitably means that in an intellectual and an emotional way I am still engaging with Cornelius. It is a tangible way in which I can continue to invite him to enter my musical life.[9]

By offering accessibility as well as extreme complexity, Cardew's *magnum opus* demonstrates its inherently democratic nature. No performer is turned away; through *Treatise* everyone can make music – from the tentative beginner to the awe-inspiring David Tudor – bringing a musical utopia tantalisingly within reach. For whatever its illustrious status in the field of composition, *Treatise* does not belong to that category of arcane 'modern' scores. One does not pore over the score in order to intuit Cardew's 'meaning'; it means what the performer, or would-be performer 'sees'. As Eddie Prévost remarked, 'An interpreter of *Treatise* is drawn to the work because there is something within its weft and warp which fascinates.'[10]

I think we have been in the comfort zone long enough.

When we move into the 1970s, the decade of revolutionary activism, *Treatise* was seen by Cardew from a completely new, Maoist perspective, as an object of criticism and rejection. So now I want to raise some of the issues which were dominant among Cardew's concerns during that last decade as he sought to grapple with a new, radical cultural agenda and the commitment and sacrifices it demanded of him.

In a note discussing the genesis of *Treatise* in his book *Stockhausen Serves Imperialism*, Cardew refers to his work as a graphic designer, when he was obliged, through financial circumstances, to pursue music as a spare-time activity. It was during one of these periods of work that he conceived and worked on *Treatise*. This, in his view, accounted for the 'escapist' nature of the composition, and he describes it as a 'fantasy' to which, at the time, he attached 'vast importance'. *Treatise* is characterised and dismissed as an 'obstacle' which 'prevents the establishment of communication between the musicians and the audience'. Moreover, it peddles an inaccurate reflection of our knowledge of the world, its forms of expression; *Treatise* is 'contradictory and incoherent'. Cardew writes:

> Summer changes to winter, iron ore is changed into steel, a sequence of notes can be changed into a melody, but a tree can never be changed into a saucer of milk. Not in the real world.[11]

No, of course, not in the real world – but indubitably in the artist's flight of imagination, a tree *can* be transformed into a saucer of milk (we may recall the great myths and popular fairy tales, such as *Alice in Wonderland* and the extravagance and wildness of Lewis Carroll's imagination, which Cardew had admired so much). Such a licence, to allow and encourage the imagination to run riot, does not guarantee a meaningful outcome, but to claim that 'on a very fundamental level, it is distorting reality, propagating lies, wrong ideas, about the world' is to attach a significance to such activity that it hardly merits. We all day-dream, we all turn truth upside down, logic inside out, often involuntarily; perhaps such mental activity has a therapeutic value; it may even be the midwife of the birth of a work of art.

Cardew's, and his Party's, insistence on the 'scientific method' was the complete antithesis of his earlier view. Until his espousal of Marxism-Leninism, it was not the scientific 'validity' of musical theories that was of importance or relevance to Cardew; it was the way in which any musical manifestation affected the lives of those who practised and listened to it. Indeed, he was sceptical of the usefulness of 'science'; when we try, for example, to describe the impression a piece of music makes on us; it might be necessary to enter other areas of speculative discourse, but rarely science. Like Wittgenstein, he held the view, at that time, that the aesthetic creations of the human mind enjoy a precious immunity from scientific analysis.

'Nothing is more *conservative* than science,' Wittgenstein once said. 'Science lays down railway tracks.'[12]

And in 1974, Cardew could write: 'Faith in the Party is a scientific matter'![13] An embarrassing oxymoron, if ever there was.

It was as if accountability to the Party was an ongoing obligation from which even science could not escape. Science had to be partisan. We cannot help but recall Engels's potent reminder: 'But how young the whole of human history still is, and how ridiculous it would be to attempt to ascribe any absolute validity to our present views.'[14]

Certainly good art tends to have a longer shelf life than good science.

But at that time, the Party was suspicious of all artistic manifestations – most of which were neither Party political nor scientific. Moreover, art is notoriously promiscuous (consider the history of Beethoven's Ninth) and tends to resist long-term relationships; it is difficult to harness and control works of art – that is, to circumscribe their field of operation and influence. The Party did not want art; it wanted only those cultural artefacts which would serve its needs. It demanded of its cultural work that it should be 'educational', that it should be 'scientific', that it should expose the iniquities of monopoly capitalism and expound the Marxist-Leninist solution. Cardew duly obliged. His political songs were not 'art'; they were largely political tracts set to music, and music *per se* is not art. Art, and *Treatise*, invite multi-meaning responses, which at that time was problematic. Since he could not control those responses, Cardew attacked the source. And attacking the source involved a confrontation with 'content', its immanence and provenance: the way sounds are sewn together, layered, juxtaposed, contrasted; the way they are presented instrumentally, formally, structurally; the way they influence and manipulate people, and so forth. Cardew's judgment was dismissive: 'Artistic thinking these days is an endless process of finessing. Without interest,' he wrote. Gerhard Richter said the same thing in 1975: 'A mindlessly proliferating activity that is becoming ever less committed.'[15]

The successful artist in our society is a true 'flower of evil', Cardew wrote.

So does the *way* we are taught Art, and its function in society, discourage us from acting swiftly to combat injustice on the streets, in our daily lives? What is the relation between Art and physical reality, between fiction and responsible truth (i.e. imagining?) which may produce the germs of evasion and corruption in the aesthetic and intellectual act itself? And what of the bondings between art and barbarism? The humanities and the inhuman. There is no document of civilisation which is not at the same time a document of barbarism, Walter Benjamin reminded us. We should not let them get away with it.

In an interview with Cardew, Adrian Jack suggests that if a magnificent building had been the home of 'a particularly vicious Renaissance family', we might now appreciate it for its 'aesthetic qualities'. Cardew contends that 'you won't like it, because of what it stands for'. When Jack ripostes that it is possible to 'divorce its aesthetic qualities from its function', Cardew's rejoinder was unequivocal: 'Well, I would never want to, you see.'[16]

People have spoken of the irrelevance, indeed the obscenity of artistic endeavour in the light of the unspeakable banalities of 20th-century history. Tucked away in the back cover of Cardew's 1973/74 journal is a sheet of notes on Hegel's *Aesthetics*. It ends: 'A question to be discussed: Art in the sense that it developed with the bourgeoisie to its great heights; will Art in this sense be carried over and developed by the Proletariat in its own interests. Or will the mode of Art associated with bourgeois philosophy (Hegel) pass away with the bourgeoisie? IMPORTANT.'

Of all the people I have known, Cardew was the one most entitled to ask that question.

People say there is a time and place for everything. For Cardew, the time is now, the place is everywhere.

Over 300 years ago, the Digger Gerrard Winstanley penned these words, which surely resonated in Cardew's thoughts:

> Yet my mind was not at rest, because nothing was acted, and thoughts run in me that words and writings were all nothing and must die, for action is the life of all, and if thou dost not act, thou dost nothing.[17]

1   Cornelius Cardew, 'Treatise: Working Notes, 8th Feb '63', *Treatise Handbook* (London: Hinrichson Edition Ltd, Edition Peters, 1971), p.iii.

2   Cornelius Cardew, 'Treatise: Working Notes, 28th Sept '63', ibid., p.iv.

3   Cornelius Cardew, 'Notation – Interpretation, etc.' TEMPO, Summer 1961, in Eddie Prévost (ed.), *Cornelius Cardew (1936–1981): A Reader* (Harlow, UK: Copula, 2006), p.11.

4   Cornelius Cardew, 'Treatise: Résumé of pre-publication performances', in ibid., p.114.

5   Cornelius Cardew, *Treatise Handbook*, in ibid., p.x.

6   Cornelius Cardew, ibid., p.xii.

7   Ibid., p.i.

8   Eddie Prévost, in John Tilbury, *Cornelius Cardew (1936–1981): A Life Unfinished* (Harlow, UK: Copula, 2008), p.316.

9   Letter from Prévost to Tilbury, 2 June 1994, quoted in ibid., p.252.

10   Ibid., p.253.

11   Cornelius Cardew, *Stockhausen Serves Imperialism* (London: Latimer New Dimensions, 1974), p.84.

12   The author is referring to an observation of Rush Rhees, 'Postscript' in his ed. *Recollections of Wittgenstein* (Oxford: Oxford University Press, 1984), p.102.

13   Cornelius Cardew, Journal, April–July 1974, dated 19 May, quoted in John Tilbury, *A Life Unfinished*, p.693.

14   Frederick Engels, *Anti-Dühring* (Moscow: Foreign Languages Publishing House, 1959), p.158.

15   John Tilbury, *A Life Unfinished*, p.665.

16   Cornelius Cardew – interviewed by Adrian Jack, Music and Musicians, May 1975, reprinted in Eddie Prévost (ed.), *Cornelius Cardew (1936–1981): A Reader*, p.236

17   'Gerrard Winstanley (Digger)', in Christopher Hampton (ed.), *A Radical Reader* (Harmondsworth: Penguin, 1984), p.231 (footnote).

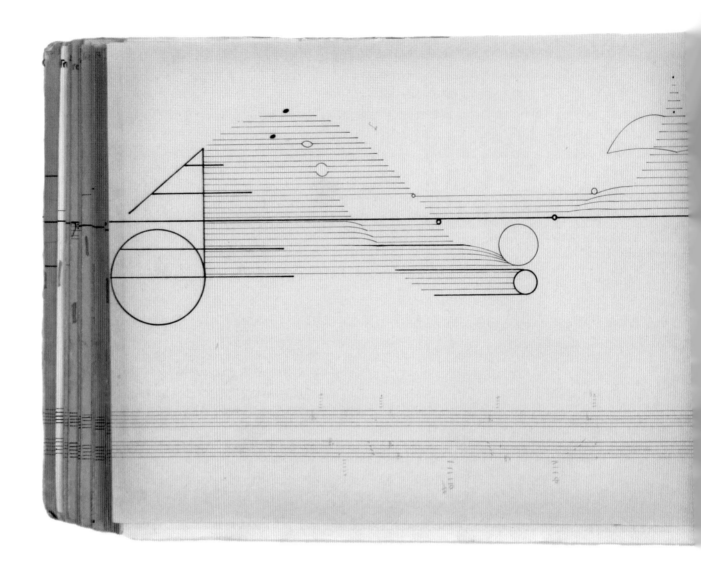

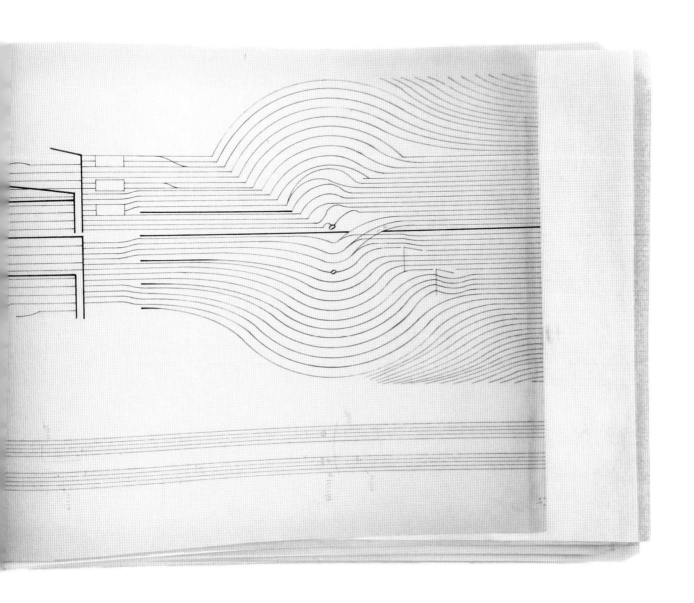

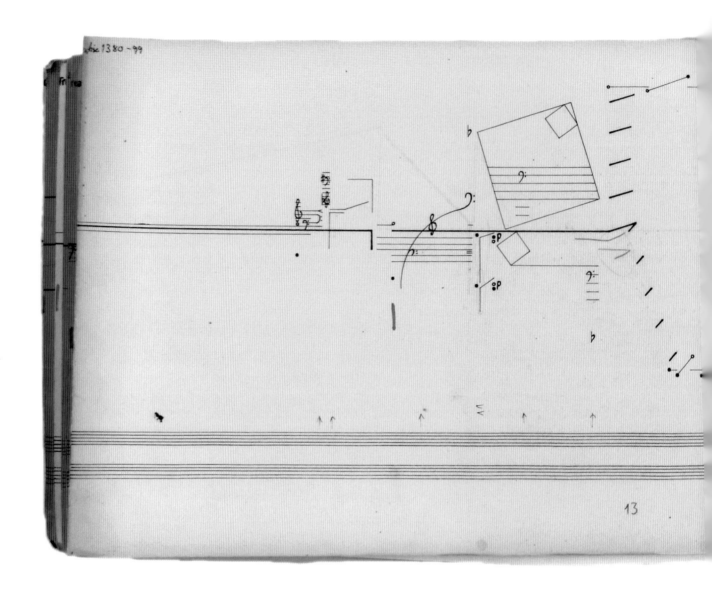

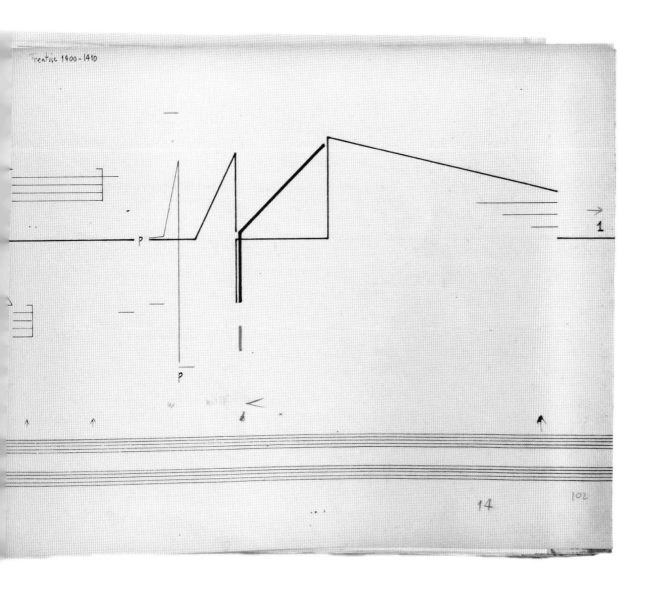

14   102

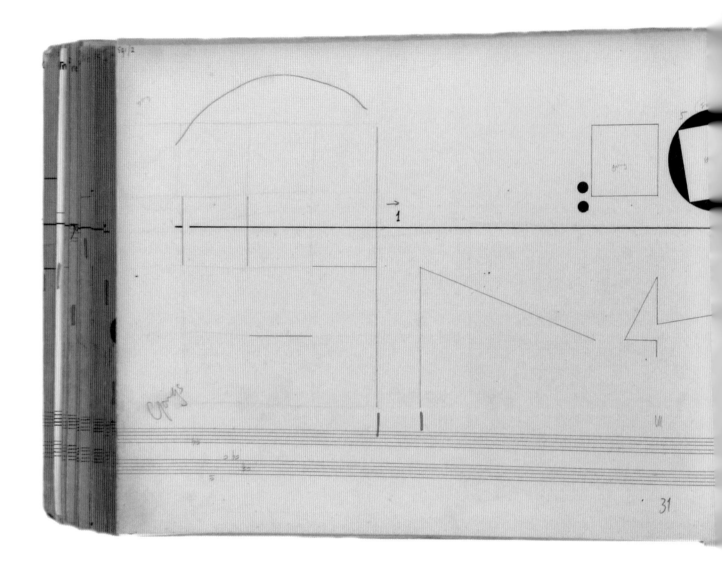

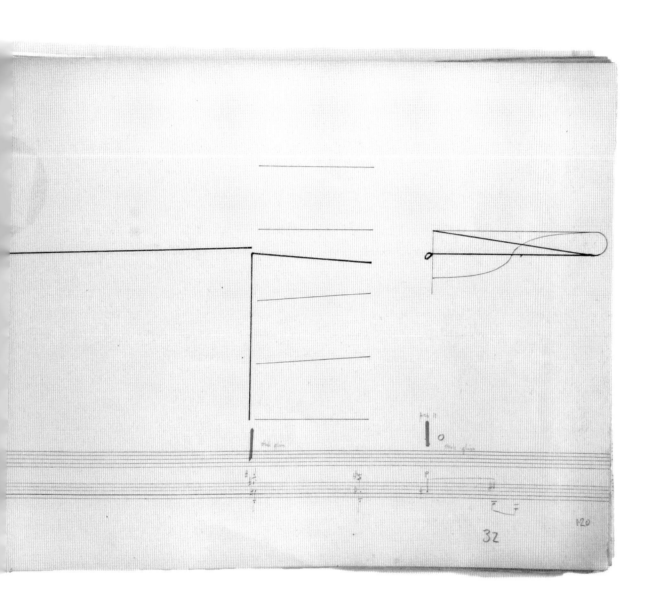

32

120

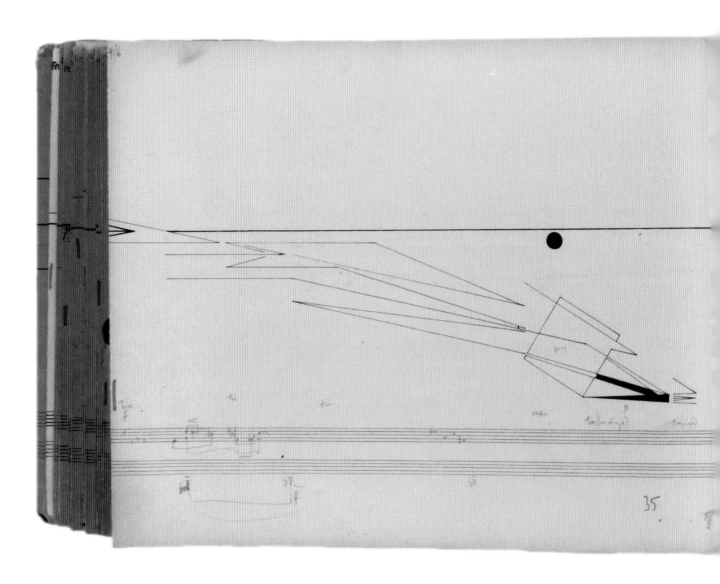

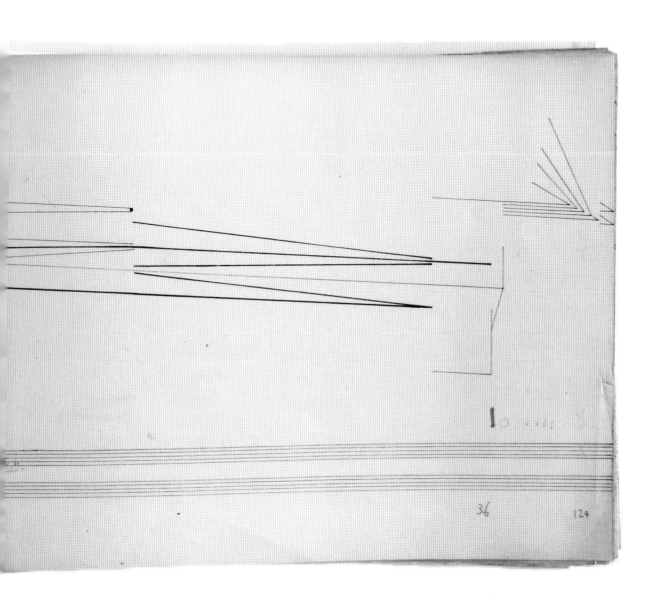

36   124

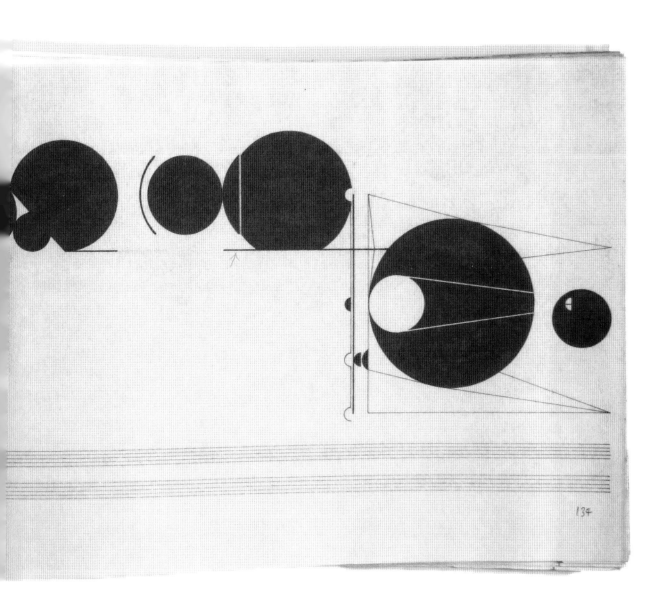

134

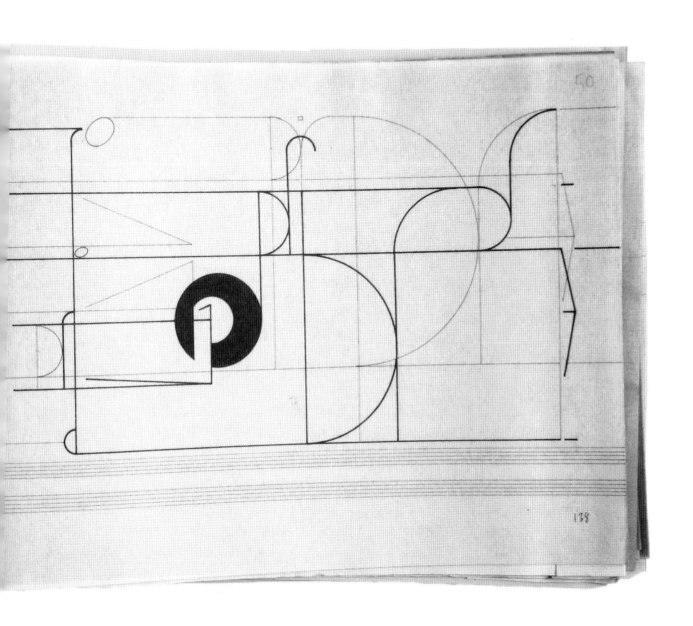

138

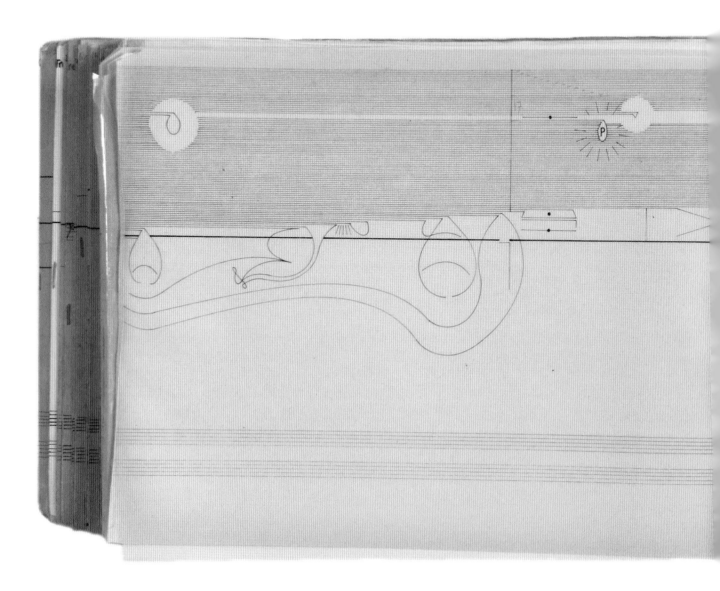

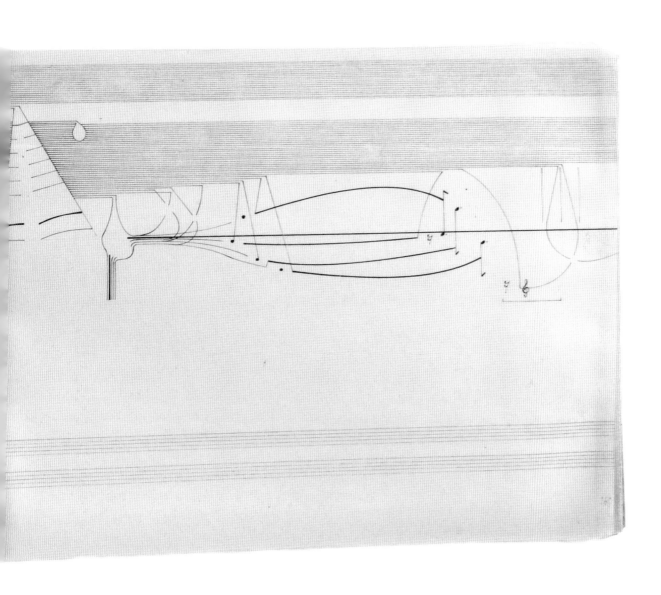

Cornelius Cardew Biography

John Tilbury

Cornelius Cardew was born in 1936. He was educated musically as a chorister at Canterbury Cathedral (1943–50), and at the Royal Academy of Music (RAM; 1953–7) where he studied Composition (with Howard Ferguson), piano (with Percy Waller) and cello. He received a RAM Scholarship to study electronic music in Cologne (1957–8), and worked as assistant to Karlheinz Stockhausen (1958–60), collaborating with him in the composition of *Carré for Four Choruses and Orchestras*. In 1961 he returned to London, took a course in graphic design, and until 1970 worked intermittently as a graphic artist. In 1964 he received an Italian Government bursary to study in Rome with Goffredo Petrassi.

From 1966 to 1971, he was a member of the free improvisation group AMM. He was elected Fellow of the Royal Academy of Music in 1966, and was appointed Professor of Composition there in 1967. From 1966 to 1967 he was associate at the Centre for Creative and Performing Arts at the State University of New York at Buffalo, NY, working on the graphic score *Treatise* (1963–7). In 1968 he began teaching an experimental music class at Morley College, London. His work there with other experimental musicians, and in particular work on a section of *The Great Learning*, led to the formation in 1969 of the Scratch Orchestra, a large experimental group. His concern to get to grips with what was really happening in the world, and his work to develop music in opposition to both commercialism and elitism, led him in 1971 to begin to take up Marxist-Leninist ideas. He subjected the negative aspects of his earlier work (including *The Great Learning*), and that of Stockhausen and Cage, to serious criticism, resulting later in the book *Stockhausen Serves Imperialism* (1974). In 1973 he received a grant from the City of West Berlin to live and work there for a year. Returning to London, he was active in the formation of People's Liberation Music, a revolutionary rock band, and ran a workshop-class at Goldsmiths College entitled 'Songs for Our Society' (1975–7). He toured and lectured extensively and in 1974 produced the 'Thälmann Sonata', the first in a series of major piano works. In 1975 he played a leading role in uniting democratic artists in the formation of the Progressive Cultural Association. He developed as a revolutionary Communist fighter for the people's cause, and in 1979 he was a founding member and member of the Central Committee of the Revolutionary Communist Party of Britain (Marxist-Leninist). He participated militantly in the democratic struggles of the people, was imprisoned in 1980 for his part in opposing a National Front Demonstration in Camberwell, and was elected as the General Secretary of the People's Democratic Front at its founding Conference in 1981. He participated in many festivals of popular culture including a series of concerts for youth across Canada in 1979, the 4th International Anti-Imperialist, Anti-Fascist Youthcamp in 1980, and the 1st International Sports and Cultural Festival in Vancouver in 1981. In September 1981, he began a Master's Degree in Musical Analysis at King's College, London. On 13 December 1981, he was killed, near to his home in Leyton, East London, by a hit-and-run driver.

Kate Macfarlane is a curator and Co-Founder and Co-Director of The Drawing Room, London, a non-profit organisation that explores ideas around contemporary drawing and makes them visible in the public domain. Published writing includes 'Investigating the Status of Drawing' in Tania Kovats (ed.), *The Drawing Book* (London: Black Dog Publishing, 2005); 'Drawing off the page', in Angela Lammert, Carolin Meister, Jan-Philipp Frühsorge, Andreas Schalhorn (eds.), *Räume der Zeichnung* (Berlin: Akademie der Künste, 2007), and contributions to The Drawing Room publications.

The Otolith Group was formed in 2002 by London-based artists Kodwo Eshun and Anjalika Sagar. Their works include the films *Otolith I* (2003), *Otolith II* (2007), *Nervus Rerum* (2008), the 13-monitor installation *Inner Time of Television* (2007), the curation of the exhibition *The Ghosts of Songs: The Film Art of The Black Audio Collective*, exhibited at FACT, Liverpool and Arnolfini, Bristol in 2007 and the co-curation of *Three Early Films: Harun Farocki* at Cubitt (2009) and *Against What? Against Whom?* (2009), in collaboration with Tate Modern and Raven Row (2009).

Michael Parsons has been active as a composer and performer since the mid-l960s. In 1969 he was co-founder with Cornelius Cardew and Howard Skempton of the Scratch Orchestra. During the 1970s and 1980s, he participated in mixed-media projects with the London Musicians' Collective, including the staged work *Expedition to the North Pole* (1984), which he devised and presented with Max Eastley.

Dr Andrea Phillips is Reader in Fine Art and Director, Curating Architecture, Goldsmiths, University of London. Her research interests focus on: contemporary art, architecture and current socio-political thought; movement, mobility and fluidity in contemporary art and political philosophy; connections between curating and socio-political activities of constructing, organising, and caring for transnational space; concepts of distribution in art, architecture and politics; Rancière, Alain Badiou and the political in art; Saskia Sassen, Ulrich Beck, David Harvey and economy *vis-à-vis* art.

Adrian Rifkin is a professor of Art Writing at Goldsmiths, University of London. On first coming to London in the late 1960s, he hung out with the New Music crowd and, while never a musician, acquired some of their habits of taking chance combined with quixotic rigour and militancy, both political and quietist. See http://qai-savoir.net.

Rob Stone writes on the Delphic histories of sound and architectural space, and the aesthetics of modern urban sociability. He completed his doctorate in 1998 on the impact of suburbanisation on modernist cultural theory in Britain, and has since curated exhibitions in art museums around Europe. Previously of the Department of Visual Cultures and the Centre for Research Architecture at Goldsmiths, University of London, he is currently Senior Research Fellow in the Department of Art at Middlesex University, and Adjunct Professor in the Department of Art History, Visual Art and Theory at the University of British Columbia. He lives in London and Vancouver. His book *Auditions: Architecture and Aurality* will be published by MIT Press soon.

John Tilbury is a British pianist and considered one of the foremost interpreters of Morton Feldman's music. He was closely associated with Cornelius Cardew with whom he first performed in January 1960 and who wrote *Volo Solo* (for a virtuoso performer of any instrument) for him in 1965. He later became a prominent member of the Scratch Orchestra and wrote *Cornelius Cardew (1936–1981): A Life Unfinished* (2008). His numerous recordings include works by John Cage, Morton Feldman, Howard Skempton, Christian Wolff and Cornelius Cardew.

Founded in 1994 by two AIDS activists in Los Angeles, **Ultra-red**, in collaboration with social justice movements, conduct investigations where sound is both the medium and the site of inquiry. With nine members located in North American and Europe, the collective produce recordings, performances, workshops, radio broadcasts and installations. Ultra-red's investigations have been hosted by institutions such as Los Angeles Contemporary Exhibitions, Art Gallery of Ontario, Tate Britain, and Serpentine Gallery, and have received support from Durfee Foundation (Los Angeles) and Fritt Ord Foundation (Oslo). Ultra-red curate the online record label and archive, Public Record (www.publicrec.org).

Grant Watson is curator at M HKA, Antwerp. Recent exhibitions include *Textiles: Art and the Social Fabric*, M HKA (2009); *Nasreen Mohamedi: Reflections on Indian Modernism* (curated with Suman Gopinath, 2009), Office for Contemporary Art, Norway, Milton Keynes Gallery, UK, Lunds Konsthall, Sweden, Kunsthalle Basel, Switzerland; *Santhal Family: Positions around an Indian Sculpture,* M HKA (2008). He was previously Curator of Visual Arts at Project Arts Centre, Dublin.

* Archive of Horace Cardew, gifted to the British Library, London. Some material is available at the British Music Information Centre, London.

** Archive of Brigid and Laurie Scott-Baker

Play for Today: Cornelius Cardew

Published by The Drawing Room, London,
UK and Museum van Hedendaagse Kunst
Antwerpen (M HKA), Belgium

© The Drawing Room, except where noted.

All rights reserved. No part of this publication
may be reproduced, stored in a retrieval system
or transmitted in any form or by any means
without the prior permission of the publisher.

ISBN 978-0-9558299-1-8

Edited by Kate Macfarlane, Rob Stone
and Grant Watson
Copy Edited by Tom Cobbe
Designed by Marit Münzberg
Printed by Graphicom, Italy

Middlesex
University

LOTTERY FUNDED

Exhibition venue and dates:

06 June 2008 – 31 August 2008
Museum van Hedendaagse Kunst Antwerpen
(M HKA)
Leuvenstraat 32
2000 Antwerp
Belgium
T +32 (0)3 260 99 99
F +32 (0)3 216 24 86
info@muhka.be
www.muhka.be

05 November – 13 December 2009
The Drawing Room
Tannery Arts
Brunswick Wharf
55 Laburnum Street
London E2 8BD
UK
+ 44 (0)20 7729 5333
mail@drawingroom.org.uk
www.drawingroom.org.uk

Tannery Arts Ltd, Industrial & Provident Society, Reg. No. 29034R

The Drawing Room Directors: Mary Doyle,
Kate Macfarlane, Katharine Stout.
Administrator: Paula Naughton.
Interns (January – November 2009):
Nadege Derderian, Assunta Ruocco,
Mathilda Strang, Aislinn White.
The Drawing Room Advisory Board:
David Austen, Peter Jenkinson OBE, Cornelia
Parker, Andrew Renton, Peter St John, Jeni
Walwin, Grant Watson and Sigrid Wilkinson.
The Drawing Room Patrons: Elizabeth Bauza,
Marie Elena Angulo & Henry Zarb, Mina Park.
Corporate Patrons: John Jones.

Greg Bright   LABYRINTH II

(NB A fotostat of the maze in the endpapers of this book may be used for performances of this piece)

Place a large 2-space paper labyrinth on the head of a large drum.

Players: One 'Tracer' and any number of 'Watchers'.

WATCHERS: These should be seated around the drum comfortably, in a similar manner to the Tracer (e.g. Tracer sits on floor; Watchers sit on floor. Tracer sits on chair; Watchers sit on chairs), with a good view of the maze. All Watchers have a glass of water from which they may drink at any time, with one exception (ie there is one glassless Watcher). All their concentration should focus on the Tracer's journey around the maze; they may close their eyes and listen to the quiet scratching from time to time.

The Watcher without a glass has the task of signaling the passage of time. He should have an ostensibly silent watch or clock and a sound producing article (e.g. gong), which should be neither quiet nor loud, and should make a sound suitable to the proceedings. He should make a single sound at each marked point in time. (e.g. one beat of a gong; one drop of a handful of coins). The time should be marked off in an arithmetical progression where the factor by which each term increases should itself be in an arithmetical progression.

Example: original factor $\equiv 2$
            secondary factor $\equiv 1$
            1st term $\equiv 3$

Then (taking one minutes   1 unit)

1st sound is made at 3 minutes after the beginning.

The 2nd sound at (3 mins + original factor, ie 2) 5 minutes after 1st sound.

3rd sound at $(5 + [2 + 1] *) = 8$ minutes after 2nd sound.

4th sound at $(8 + [3 + 1]\ ) = 12$ minutes after 3rd sound

5th sound at $(12 + [4 + 1]\ ) = 17$ minutes after 4th sound etc. — the sounds thus becoming less and less frequent.

(* the secondary factor)

N.B. (i) Timing should commence approximately when the Tracer draws the match. (ii) Any measure of time (e.g. 1 sec, 30 sec, 1 min, n mins) may be taken as one unit. (iii) The numerical progression may be worked out before or during the performance, or a combination of both.

The TRACER: After settling in his position, he should take a match (preferably new from an unopened box) and, using the wooden end, begin tracing his way through the labyrinth. He should barely pause to rest. His labours must continue until he reaches the end of the labyrinth. While the Watchers sit in contemplative calm, the Tracer's eyes may be watering from the strain; beads of sweat may appear on his forehead.

— NOT A WORD IS UTTERED THROUGHOUT —